MW01658425

FIRST STEPS
Discipling Your Child

Helping your child know, love, & follow Jesus

SPECIFICITY

First Steps: Discipling Your Child

Helping your child know, love, & follow Jesus

ISBN 10: 0-9790868-2-5

ISBN 13: 978-0-9790868-2-3

Acknowledgments

Editorial Direction: Grant Edwards

Art Direction: Barbara Edwards

Our *First Steps: Discipling Your Child* team includes:

Jody Brolsma, Shawn Keefer, Mikal Keefer, Andrea Zimmerman

Specificity Publications © 2007

For more information contact:

Discipling Another to Love Jesus

2301 Valley Loop Drive

Springfield, Ohio 45504

(937) 322-5381

www.disciplinganother.com

Unless otherwise noted, Scripture passages are from the New Century Version.

Copyright © 1987, 1988, 1991 by Thomas Nelson, Inc. Used by permission. All rights reserved.

Foreword

Today, more than ever, children need the right foundation to grow in Christ—and their parents can best provide that foundation.

Daunting task, isn't it? What is the right foundation? What should parents teach or not teach? Do they have the time? What comes first?

Answering those questions inspired *First Steps for Children* and its companion website at www.disciplinganother.com.

First Steps for Children is a ten-week adventure between parents and children. These sessions give a child what's needed to have a strong Christian faith. A solid foundation that lasts a lifetime.

As this program was developed, we understood the best way to communicate the material was relationally—so as parents disciple their children, they'll grow closer. And both parents and children will grow closer to Jesus.

I wouldn't have much to say about discipling children had I not discipled my own children—Megan, Emily, and Matthew. If I'd had this book when I was discipling my kids, they wouldn't have endured so much trial and error!

I want to thank my wife, Barbara, for her patience and clarity of thought. And her willingness to smile when most would frown.

For years, Doug and Jayn Carson have faithfully supported our efforts to help individuals and churches embrace discipleship—and we thank them.

This book was initially supported both in prayer and financially by Christian and Sandra Victor. They're truly faithful partners in seeing a vision for discipling children...and doing something about it.

Mikal Keefer and I developed *First Steps for Children*, and then Mikal's top-notch crew of writers performed the miracle that is this book. I thank them.

It's my prayer that parents will disciple their children—to embrace the adventure God has entrusted to them. As they do, this book will be an encouraging, step-by-step guide.

Adults need to be discipled, too! Check out *First Steps for Adults* and a companion book outlining the essentials of effective discipleship, *Swimming Lessons*, by visiting www.disciplinganother.com.

Table of Contents

Introduction for Parents

Everything you need to know to launch an amazing, life-changing discipling relationship with your child.

When my first child was born, I was *amazed* by how many phone numbers I suddenly needed to keep handy.

There was the pediatrician, of course, plus a nurses' hotline to help us decide if stubborn rashes on my daughter's backside required doctor visits. And as we added more children our list of phone numbers grew longer.

A pediatric dentist. An orthodontist. Two optometrists. Enough school nurses to staff a moderately sized hospital.

And every year there were new teachers. Plus coaches, band directors, and camp counselors. Toss in Sunday school teachers, midweek leaders, scout masters, and a children's pastor, and Barbara and I didn't have a village helping raise our kids—there was a full-sized *city* involved.

But one piece of the puzzle was ours alone.

We decided *we'd* see that our children were given the tools to grow in their relationship with Jesus. We welcomed help from other Christian adults and church programs, but at the end of the day it was our job—and our joy—to disciple our kids.

That you're reading this book tells me you've made a similar decision.

Good for you.

Because, in reality, you're *already* discipling your child.

Do as I Say...*and* as I Do

Studies confirm the obvious: parents are the primary faith-shapers in the lives of their children. The biggest influence in your child's spiritual development isn't a Sunday school teacher or pastor. It's not the religion teacher at school.

Studies confirm the obvious: parents are the primary faith-shapers in the lives of their children. The biggest influence in your child's spiritual development isn't a Sunday school teacher or pastor. It's not the religion teacher at school.

Use these next 10 weeks to let God deepen your life in him, too. If you've failed to honor him in some way, let your child see and hear you repent, be forgiven, and move on in faithfulness.

It's you.

For better or worse, children learn how to live by watching their parents. Kids soak up our attitudes, watching our example.

Scary thought, huh? You know how often your child has seen you at your worst.

But consider these words from Deuteronomy 6:6-8...

"These commandments that I give you today are to be upon your hearts. Impress them on your children. Talk about them when you sit at home and when you walk along the road, when you lie down and when you get up."

God *intended* for you to provide the chief spiritual example for your child. And the place of greatest impact isn't some special occasion or church retreat—it's daily life.

You're the person best able to give your child the heart and skills to engage Jesus in a lifelong friendship. God has placed you in a spot of enormous influence...given you a tender heart toward your child...and provided the power of his Holy Spirit to enable you to bring up your child to know, love, and honor him.

And knowing all that—you're probably terrified.

There's little as daunting as the thought of discipling your own child...for two reasons.

1. Your child knows you...the *real* you.

Your child knows you don't pray as often as you should. That you can go a week without cracking your Bible. Isn't it hypocritical to encourage your child to grow in areas where you, too, could use improvement?

Nope...because you'll *never* be a perfect example for your child to follow. There will *always* be areas in your life where you need to grow.

Use these next ten weeks to let God deepen your life in him, too. If you've failed to honor him in some way, let your child see and hear you repent, be forgiven, and move on in faithfulness.

It's a powerful example.

2. You're not quite sure what to do.

Relax...we've got you covered.

"Discipling" is the process of teaching a young Christian those things they need to know to be established in their faith. It's helping someone fall in love with Jesus.

And it's easier than you think.

Young Christians—like your child—only need to know a few things to grow in their relationship with Jesus. They're the same things needed to know to grow in *any* relationship, so most of what you'll do is help your child establish habits and patterns that make for growing friendships.

The principles in this book are biblical, practical, and proven. We've seen them set young believers on the course of lifelong spiritual growth thousands of times, in churches around the world.

And we'll walk you through the process step by step.

So take a deep breath and get ready for an adventure—one you'll share with your child. One that draws your child deeper into a loving relationship with God. One that sets your child on a path that will change his or her life for eternity.

"Discipling" is the process of teaching a young Christian those things they need to know to be established in their faith. It's helping someone fall in love with Jesus.

First, some practical stuff...

Before you dive into the first session, nail down these details:

Get the right Bibles

Give your child a Bible appropriate for his or her reading level. New "children's Bibles" loaded with bells and whistles hit the market constantly, so there are plenty of choices.

But *don't* pick a Bible based on extra material or a flashy cover. Pick a Bible that fits your child's reading level. That's what matters most.

The *New International Readers Version* is based on the popular *New International Version* and designed for a typical 3rd-grade reader. Slightly more demanding is the *New Century Version*, designed for

Your influence in guiding your child can't be overemphasized. The blessing you'll pray mirrors a practice often seen in the Old Testament—and that has a huge impact on your child.

4th-grade readers. The *New International Version* is easily comprehended by a typical 8th-grade reader.

When you get a Bible for your child, buy an identical copy for yourself. That way you and your child will be on the same page—literally!

Plan for Week 10

On Week 10 we suggest you treat your child to a special time with you. You'll determine what to do, but expect it to cost a few dollars. Plan now so your budget can absorb the shock.

Blessed to be a blessing

You'll pray a blessing over your child in week 10.

Each week, as you work through this book, you'll see a "Blessed to be a Blessing" section. In each is a quote and some questions that help you sort out who your child is—and what calling God may have in mind for your child.

Your influence in guiding your child can't be overemphasized. The blessing you'll pray mirrors a practice often seen in the Old Testament—and that has a huge impact on your child.

So it's important you "study" your child throughout this discipling process. Ask God how to speak into your child's life...how God's wired your child for service in the Kingdom...how you can best cooperate with God's purposes for your child.

Schedule 45 minutes per week

Put time for discipling in your schedule, your child's schedule, on the family schedule—everywhere. Treat this time as untouchable.

Kids are accustomed to being shuffled around for their parents' convenience. When you treat this appointment as important, that sends a message: what you're talking about is important, too.

Show up for your discipling times refreshed, relaxed, and unhurried. Discipling your child isn't something you cram in as you're dashing off to something more important; it *is* what's more important.

Do your homework

Several times your child will be asked to learn a memory verse or do some reading. Do the same—and not at the last minute. If possible, arrange for your child to *see* you doing the prep work.

Put time for discipling in your schedule, your child's schedule, on the family schedule—everywhere. Treat this time as untouchable.

Arrange Internet access

You'll find additional, downloadable discipling material on our website for your child to enjoy—free. Activities, puzzles, application challenges—there's something for each weekly session.

Please note: we don't collect any information about or from your child. We simply want to provide "do it myself" reinforcement materials for your child to use between discipling sessions.

Check us out at www.disciplinganother.com and take advantage of these fun, session-reinforcing extras.

Read ahead

Look ahead at the coming sessions. Get a sense of where you're headed, supplies you'll need, and think about how to best engage your child in the sessions.

This is important stuff—don't let the time you meet with your child be the first time you read a session.

Decide what sort of child you're discipling

Take a look at the chart on page 14. We've described three general personality categories, and odds are good one of them most closely resembles your child.

Each week we'll suggest activities designed to appeal to each of these personalities. Why? Because children don't all learn the same way—and you want your child to engage with discipling as naturally and deeply as possible. It makes sense to tailor the material to your child.

Feel free to use any or all of the activities—they all make the same point and cover the same material. It's your choice!

What you're doing has eternal consequences. Pray daily for wisdom and patience. For faithfulness. For your child and yourself. Ask others to pray specifically for you, and update what you want covered in prayer as you move through these sessions.

Pray–a *lot*

What you're doing has eternal consequences. Pray daily for wisdom and patience. For faithfulness. For your child and yourself. Ask others to pray specifically for you, and update what you want covered in prayer as you move through these sessions.

If you're part of a group...

We suggest if you and your child are part of a larger group that you begin with a launch party. Your pastor or children's pastor will probably arrange this, and we've provided an outline in chapter 11. There's also a wrap-up celebration in chapter 12.

If you're part of a group, you'll make use of the First Steps Baton. But if you're doing this program alone, you don't need to miss out on this touching, memorable symbol. Visit us at www.disciplinganother.com and we'll help you get these inexpensive symbols of discipling.

Read chapters 11 and 12 for a clear understanding of how to use the First Steps Baton with your child.

If you're flying solo...

Download and print a copy of the First Steps Covenant. You'll find it at www.disciplinganother.com. At your first discipleship meeting with your child, read and sign it. It's your agreement about what you'll do together.

Roll up the Covenant and place it inside your baton.

Once you've done that, take a deep breath. It's time to begin.

You've scheduled your 10 sessions, have the right tools in hand, and you've dedicated this time to God.

Get ready for some fun!

How to Personalize These Discipling Sessions

Your child's unique! Here's how to tailor these discipling sessions so they connect with your child and speak to his or her temperament.

God's wired children to be unique—and we're glad about that! The world would be a poorer place if every child had the same strengths, the same weaknesses, and liked the same flavor of ice cream.

Some kids are naturally energetic...others patient...and some enjoy details, while others are "big picture" visionaries. Kids come with different temperaments—and different learning styles.

Asked to do a project, Jackie jumps right in, figuring it out as she goes. Bob carefully reads all the directions first. And Sue wants to talk through how to proceed; that's how she processes information best.

Before you begin discipling your child, it's good to ask this question: what's the temperament of your child?

Some kids are naturally energetic...others patient...and some enjoy details, while others are "big picture" visionaries. Kids come with different temperaments—and different learning styles.

Three temperament styles

Look at the chart below and decide which of the three toys best describes the child you're discipling. It won't be an exact match—God's wired your child to be unique, remember—but you'll see similarities.

There's no "right" or "wrong" temperament. And the goal isn't to label your child. Yet, if you've got a Grade-A, Bona-Fide "Jigsaw Puzzle," you'll find your child learns more if you provide opportunities that play to his or her strengths. The same is true for the other temperament styles.

Check out the chart on the next page:

Temperament Styles

Look at the chart below and decide which of the three toys best describes the child you're discipling.

Jigsaw Puzzles

These children enjoy carefully coloring in every corner of the picture—the *right* way. They're capable of diving into adventure, but they seem happiest when doing detailed, orderly tasks and arranging the parts and pieces just so.

Words that describe Jigsaw Puzzles include:

- Perfectionist
- Pragmatic
- Matter-of-Fact
- Reserved
- Analytical
- Thoughtful
- Careful
- Calculated
- Restrained
- Painstaking

Superballs

Yee-hah! These spontaneous, fun-loving kids ricochet from one thing to the next, making friends and connections as they go. Passionate, positive, and seldom pooped, Superballs have two speeds: "on" and "asleep."

Words that describe Superballs include:

- Passionate
- Independent
- Verbal
- Friendly
- Easily bored
- Ringleader
- Spontaneous
- Creative
- Determined
- Enthusiastic

Teddy Bears

These sensitive, warm children may seem older than they actually are, their patience and relational abilities tacking a few years onto their chronological age. They can identify the feelings of others, and are often voted "Most Likely To Become a Diplomat" by their peers.

Words that describe Teddy Bears include:

- Tender-hearted
- Hesitant
- Sympathetic
- Non-confrontational
- Loyal
- Comfortable with routine
- Flexible
- Sympathetic
- Accepting
- Nurturing

Tending the Toybox

Which one of the toys best describe your child? Jot your answer below:

____

As you move through these discipling sessions, you'll see we've provided follow-up application activities for each temperament type. You (and your child) will decide which activities to do, but generally speaking your child will be drawn to activities designed for his or her temperament.

All of the activities reinforce the same Bible truths and spiritual development skills; they're equally effective.

But they'll *only* be effective if your child actually does the activities—so be sure to select activities that match your child's energy level and natural wiring.

SESSION 1

Welcome to the Family!

Your child has a special spot in the Family of God, and God has an adventure planned for your child. You'll discover what it is—and decide to trust Jesus!

A note from Grant

We grownups often think of children as "associate" members of the church, too young to get involved in a significant way. Too young to do ministry. Too young to make a contribution.

And we're wrong.

Jesus doesn't discriminate on the basis of age. When people enter into a relationship with him, Jesus meets them where they are—even if they're in elementary school.

If your child has accepted Jesus as Savior and Lord, there's a relationship. And if it's not nurtured, it will do what any neglected relationship does: wither away.

The next 10 weeks you won't teach your child theology or nail down doctrine. You'll *encourage a loving relationship with Jesus.* The rest of what your child needs to know—how to navigate the Bible, what communion's about, the joys of church work days—will come later.

Keep your focus on your child's *relationship with Jesus.* It's what will prompt faithful living and lifelong discipleship.

Nothing is more important than that growing friendship with Jesus.

This session you'll help your child discover that a relationship with Jesus grows deeper if we do several simple things:

- Pray
- Read the Bible
- Fellowship
- Share our faith story

The rest of the discipling sessions will help you integrate these disciplines into the life of your child...and your life, too.

Let's get started!

The Point:

Jesus wants your child to be his disciple—and to trust him.

What you'll need:

A $5 bill you don't mind losing
Pair of clean socks
Clean cloth blindfold
Earphones attached to an mp3 player or portable CD player
Lollipop (or another type of hard candy)
Several sturdy chairs
Two Bibles

Dive In

Discipler Tip

When you ask a question, pause long enough to get an answer. Don't rush to fill in a brief time of silence. Children are used to being talked *at* by grown-ups, not talked *with*. Grown-ups don't often listen carefully to children. It may take your child awhile to trust that when you ask a question, you're respectfully listening for an answer.

Find the Fiver (15 minutes)

Say: **I've got a five-dollar bill for you. It's a gift—no strings attached. I'll place it in plain sight and all you have to do is pick it up. Sound easy enough?**

Of course, this assumes that you can do a few things.

You'll need to see the bill, which is hard to do when you're wearing a blindfold. (Tie on the blindfold.)

And you have to pick it up, which is tough when you're wearing sock mittens. (Pull on the socks on your child's hands.)

I think you can *taste* money, too, so I'll put a lollipop in your mouth. (Give your child the candy.)

And just in case the bill calls out to you, I'll put these earphones on you...playing music *I* like! Once you hear the music, wait ten seconds and then go get the bill. Ready?

Place the earphones in the ears of your child, place the bill somewhere in the room, and then wait 45 seconds before removing the earphones.

Say: **So far it's not going very well. Maybe if you give up the lollipop.** Take the lollipop and wait 45 seconds.

Say: **Still not working. Tell you what: I'll take off the socks.** Do so and wait 45 seconds as your child searches.

Say: **Okay, off with the blindfold!** Your child will quickly locate the bill.

Say: **The gift is yours to keep. I wanted you to have this good gift, but it took you a while to claim it.**

Ask your child the following questions, and discuss your child's answers:

- **What made finding this gift difficult?**
- **What would have made getting this gift easier?**

Say: **I'm your parent, and I love you. I want a close, growing relationship with you. I'll give you lots of good gifts, but none are more precious than my love.**

Jesus loves you, too, and he wants a close, growing relationship with you. There are gifts he wants to give you, too.

He wants to give you an exciting life full of adventure.

He wants you to have joy.

He wants you to be with him forever in Heaven.

But no gift is more precious than his love...and the chance to follow him as his disciple.

In the next few weeks we'll talk about how to be Jesus' disciple. How to follow him. How to know and trust him. How to grow in your friendship with him.

And it's gonna be an adventure!

Discipler Tip

Notice that questions are all "open-ended." That means they can't be answered with a simple "yes" or "no." They draw out what your child really thinks and feels. Follow up answers your child gives you with additional questions, digging deeper, but always make the questions open-ended. They keep the good stuff coming!

Dig In

Why Trust Jesus? (20 minutes)

Ask your child to stand on a sturdy chair as you read the Leap of Faith Story 1 on page 24.

At the end of the story, ask your child to jump to the floor.

Discuss with your child:

- **How would it feel to leap into the darkness?**
- **What helped the friends take the leap?**

Say: **We were like those friends. We were stuck in sin with no way out. And the Bible says the price we pay for sinning is death!**

Read Romans 3:23 and Romans 6:23 aloud. If your child is able, ask your child to read the passages.

You took the leap and trusted Jesus to save you. That's great—and he's done it!

But there's another leap we need to take, too, a next step. You also have to trust Jesus enough to be his ***disciple.*** To let him be your Lord—someone you serve.

A disciple is someone who follows Jesus daily. It's not a one-time thing; it's every day, day after day. It's loving Jesus enough to go where he sends you, to do what he wants you to do.

We can be disciples...but to follow Jesus we've first got to trust him.

Let's look at four reasons we can trust Jesus.

Reason #1: Jesus knows you

Read Luke 12:6-8.

Say: **Do you know how many hairs you have on your head? Take a guess. The number depends on your hair color and age, but it's probably around 100,000. And you lose between 50 and 100 hairs every day.**

Jesus knows exactly how many you have. He knows your name. He knows everything about you—your needs, your wants. Who your friends are. What you're afraid of.

It's easier to trust someone when that person knows us...and we get to know that person.

- **Who's someone you didn't trust at first, but as you got to know each other, your trust grew?**

Reason #2: Jesus loves you

Read John 3:16 and Romans 5:8 together.

Say: **Jesus loves you with his whole heart. So much that he died in your place so you could be forgiven for the wrong things you've done.**

- **How does it feel knowing Jesus loves you that much?**

Reason #3: Jesus wants what's best for you

Read John 10:10 and Romans 8:28 together.

Say: **Jesus will never trick you or make fun of you. He will never hurt you. He wants you to grow into a person who honors God and stands firm for the Truth. That's a friend who helps you become all you can be!**

- **What's something Jesus has asked you to do?**

Reason #4: Jesus wants to be your friend forever

Read John 14:3 together.

Say: **Most of our friendships come and go. Think about your friends a few years ago. Have you added any friends since then?**

Pause to identify friendships that have lasted and faded.

Say: **Jesus wants to be your forever friend. To be a friend today, tomorrow, and always. For that to happen we have to keep growing in our friendship with him. The way to do that is to become a disciple—to know, love, and follow Jesus.**

- **What's something you know or love about Jesus?**

Ask your child to climb back on a chair. Get on a sturdy chair or stepstool yourself and read aloud Leap of Faith Story 2.

At the end of the story invite your child to jump to the floor with you.

Say: **In the next 10 weeks we'll have fun learning simple ways to know, love, and follow Jesus. That's the adventure Jesus has for you: a lifetime of following him.**

So let's get to know him better together!

Make it Mine

Shhhhh….!

Say: **This week let's jump into the adventure by trusting Jesus.**

In Matthew 6:1-4 Jesus tells us to give without expecting any applause. Jesus says God will see what we do and reward us. So this week let's give to the needy without getting any credit for it.

Discuss with your child:

• **Who do we know who's needy? What do they need? How might we help?**

It's important that you select someone to help who your child can actually see—this won't be a memorable experience if you simply send a check off to a distant mission organization.

Look for a project in the chart on page 23 that fits your child. Or, even better, work to accomplish a project selected by your child.

"TRUST IN THE LORD WITH ALL YOUR HEART AND LEAN NOT ON YOUR OWN UNDER-STANDING; IN ALL YOUR WAYS ACKNOWLEDGE HIM, AND HE WILL MAKE YOUR PATHS STRAIGHT."

—Proverbs 3:5-6

Blessed to be a Blessing

Extending trust is difficult for some people—children included. Even the people who met Jesus face to face during his earthly ministry didn't all choose to trust him.

The most convincing argument that Jesus is trustworthy is...you. Your life. If your child sees that you trust Jesus, and obey him, that says it all to your child.

So this week, be intentional about modeling discipleship. When you tell stories about your day, include those moments you chose to respond to a road-rage driver in a patient, caring way. That you did the right thing not because it was easy, but because that's what Jesus did.

Demonstrate *your* trust in Jesus and you'll see that trust reflected in your child's life.

In what ways do you demonstrate trust in Jesus?

How trusting is your child by nature? Why do you answer as you do?

What practical ways can you encourage your child's trust in Jesus this week?

"TRUST EVERYBODY, BUT CUT THE CARDS."

—Finley Peter Dunne

Pray:

Dear God, you know the power of trust. Of faith. Of taking you at your word. Give my child a deep, solid trust in you and Jesus. Show me how to help that trust take root and grow throughout my child's life. Amen.

Operation: Trust Jesus

Objective: Give something meaningful to someone in need—without getting credit for the gift.

Jigsaw Puzzles

Ask your child to design a card by hand or on a computer, then anonymously deliver the card to someone who needs encouragement.

If your child is musical, consider how to write and/or play a song or piece of music for others—without being identified as the author.

Superballs

Encourage your child to organize a group effort to meet a need.

A neighborhood food drive with the proceeds going to a specific family in need identified through your church...a community effort to clean up the property of an elderly or bedridden person... launching a prayer chain to support someone in need.

Teddy Bears

Work with your child to write an encouraging, uplifting note and get the note into the hands of a discouraged person—without the person knowing who wrote the note.

The note could be slipped into a locker or coat pocket...sent through the mail anonymously...left under a windshield wiper...or taped to a bouquet of flowers and placed where it's sure to be found.

Leap of Faith Story 1

Two friends were hiking in the mountains.

The day had been perfect—crisp and sunny. But late in the afternoon it suddenly grew dark. The friends saw storm clouds rushing toward them. The temperature dropped. Snow and sleet slashed at their thin clothes.

The friends were stuck on a rock ledge in total darkness, freezing to death. They had just enough power in a cell phone to make one call to 911.

The operator couldn't help, but patched them through to a man who said the following:

"I know right where you are. Below you about ten feet is another ledge. If you jump you'll land on it and find a cave. There's shelter from the storm and in the morning we'll get you some help."

The two friends hadn't noticed any ledge beneath them, and in the darkness they couldn't see one. Jump off the mountain and risk falling hundreds of feet to their deaths? That was asking a lot!

As their cell phone faded they asked who they were talking to and recognized his name. The voice was that of a forest ranger and expert mountain climber who'd worked in the mountains for years.

So they jumped—and found the ledge.

They lived through the night.

Leap of Faith Story 2

Two friends were living their lives in (your city here).

Most of their days were great, but sometimes they ran into hard times. Times that school or work didn't go well. Times they were angry or sad.

Sometimes they felt like they knew exactly what to do. Other times they didn't have a clue.

Every day there was a voice that called out to them. The voice said, "Trust me. I know you, so trust me. I love you, so trust me. I want what's best for you, so trust me. I want to be your friend forever, so trust me."

The friends heard the voice every morning, and every morning they had to decide if they would trust the voice. If they would listen and obey.

They knew who was speaking. It was Jesus.

So the friends had to decide: were they willing to take the leap?

SESSION 2

Friends Forever

Good news: Jesus wants to be your child's friend—now and forever. Let's get to know him and see what sort of friendship he wants to have with your child.

A note from Grant

When my son was small he was both independent and fearless...a trying combination. He was quick to dash out into the road without looking, and had several near misses.

I wanted him to stop when I called out for him to do so, and he did.

But it was important that he stop not because he *feared* me and was terrified I'd punish him. I wanted him to stop because he *loved* me and wanted to please me.

Either way he'd be safe from whatever car was barreling down the road.

But only obedience because of love would protect him later, when I wasn't around to yell out a warning.

When he sat in class knowing that others were cheating on the test—and needing to decide if he'd join them. When he was a teenager asked to attend a questionable party. When he was pressured to compromise and had to stand firm—or not.

When we obey out of fear, there's no reason to obey when the person we fear will discipline us can't see what we're doing. But when we obey out of love, we're motivated to obey always...even when we'd never be caught.

God wants us to obey out of love. To be drawn to his character out of love and not fear. That's the relationship he wants with us because that's the relationship he offers us: a loving father who expects obedience—but obedience for all the right reasons.

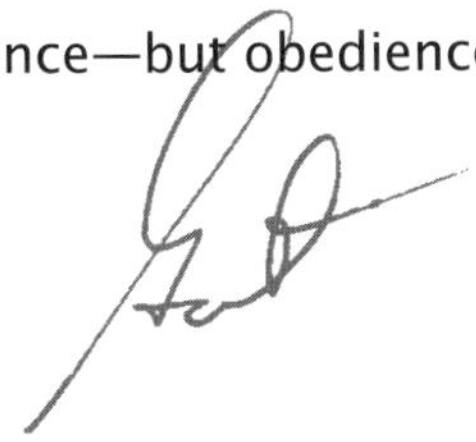

The Point:

Disciples have a loving friendship with Jesus—and that love prompts obedience.

What you'll need:

Paper and pencils
A Bible
Two key blanks from the hardware store (buy just the blanks; don't have the keys ground so they open something)

Dive In

Do as I Say (15 minutes)

Say: **It's hard to take adults seriously sometimes, isn't it? Maybe that's because adults don't always do what they ask you to do. Like taking out the trash, cleaning their rooms, cleaning up after the dog in the back yard, and obeying. You have to obey a lot of people. Who are all the people you obey?**

Allow time for your child's response.

Say: **I'm an adult. Who do you think I have to obey?**

Allow time for your child's response.

Say: **I obey my boss at work. I obey the people I love when they ask me to do things, as long as they're good things to do. But most importantly, I obey Jesus.**

Obeying Jesus is especially tough because he asks me to do things like being kind to people who aren't kind to me, and caring for people I don't even know.

But here's a great reason to take Jesus seriously: he did everything he asks us to do—even the tough stuff.

He loved people even when they were mean to him.

He was patient with his friends, even when he had to repeat himself over and over.

He felt pain—more pain than I've ever felt—when he hung on the cross.

He even died, like we'll both do one day.

And he did all these things out of obedience to God, his father.

Have your child look up and read aloud John 14:23-24.

Discuss the following:

- **Do you always obey people because you love them? Why else might you obey someone?**
- **Which do you think is most important: loving Jesus, or obeying him? Why?**

Discipler Tip

Keep an open mind. This exercise will tell you what your child thinks about the rules in your home—and why. That's good stuff! You may discover that behind what you've assumed was misbehavior is a lack of understanding... or a miscommunication.

- **Why do you think Jesus asks people who love him to do what he says?**

Say: **Jesus wants us to obey him, but not just because he's so powerful. He wants us to obey because we love him. Because we trust that he loves us and wants what's best for us.**

Disciples are followers of Jesus, and that means we need to obey Jesus. But not because we're afraid. Instead, he wants us to obey out of love!

Dig In

House Rules

Say: **Did you know that it's against the law in Massachusetts to have a duel with water pistols? And in New York City it's against the law for citizens to say hello to each other by putting their thumbs to their noses and wiggling their fingers? But even though those laws are written down, people don't often get arrested for breaking them. There are rules, and then there are RULES—the really important rules that count!**

Give your child a pencil and a piece of notebook paper. Keep a pencil and piece of paper yourself.

Say: **I want you to think of the seven biggest, most important rules in our house. The rules that get you in real trouble if you break them. Write them down on your piece of paper.**

I'm going to write down the seven rules I think are most important in our house. Then we'll compare our lists and see if they're the same. And no cheating—I won't look at your paper and you can't look at mine.

Ready? Let's take three minutes to write down the rules.

At the end of three minutes put down your pencil and ask your child to do the same. If your child couldn't come up with seven rules, that's fine—work with the rules that are there.

Discipler Tip

Your child may have made a commitment to Jesus as Savior without realizing there's a do-what-Jesus-says Lordship element to the relationship. *First Steps* will begin to bring that part of the relationship into focus.

And this program is also a great time to confirm that your child has made a commitment to Jesus. Explore that—ask your child.

Baton Prayers

In week 10 or 11 you'll share with your child what you've been praying for him or her. Take a few moments and, on a sheet of paper, write any long-term prayers you have for your child. Maybe it's to marry a believer. Or to be a faithful follower all his or her life. Whatever those requests are, write them down and then roll up the page and slip it into your baton.

Say: **Let's compare lists.**

Switch lists and see how many rules are the same on your lists.

Ask your child to explain why he selected the rules he listed. Ask if he believes each rule is a good or bad one, and why. What makes it a good or bad rule?

Do the same with your list.

When you're finished, lay down the lists.

Say: **I don't want you to obey the rules in our home because I can punish you if you don't obey the rules. I'd rather you obey rules because you want me to be happy with you and because you love me. Because you trust that I want what's best for you.**

When we obey only because we're afraid of punishment, as soon as the person who can punish us is gone, we quit obeying.

Jesus wants us to love him and obey him because of that love. I love you and want you to obey me for the same reason.

Make It Mine

Love to Obey

Say: **Here's what's tricky about obeying because of love: from the outside it looks just like obeying because you're afraid of being punished. Like lots of discipleship stuff, this is a matter of the heart.**

This week let's work on heart stuff. That's why this week I want us both to carry these key blanks.

Show your child a key that's been keyed to open a lock. Ask your child to compare the blank and keyed keys.

Say: **Your key blank won't open any locks because it hasn't been fitted to the tumblers inside a lock. For it to work on our house, or a car, it has to be shaped a certain way.**

Your key *looks* like it should work...but it won't. Sometimes we *look* like we're obeying for the right reason...but we aren't.

This week when you need to obey someone, and when I need to obey someone, let's put our hands in our pockets to feel our key blanks. The key blanks will remind us that we can choose to obey for the *right* reasons—like loving or honoring the person asking us to obey.

And as we practice obeying for the right reasons, God will shape our hearts to open to him.

Discuss with your child:

- **Would you say you're naturally obedient, disobedient, or somewhere in between? Why do you answer as you do?**
- **Where do you think you'll have the greatest challenge with obeying this week? Why?**

"THERE IS NO SHAME IN TAKING ORDERS FROM THOSE WHO THEMSELVES HAVE LEARNED TO OBEY."

—William Edward Forster

Blessed to be a Blessing

Think just because you're the grownup that you're off the hook with obedience? Far from it.

Adults struggle with obeying God, too. Every disciple deals with a desire to simply forget what God wants and to do our own thing in our own way, on our own timetable.

Take seriously your role as a disciple and discipler this week. Carry your key blank and let it remind you that while we can obey for lots of reasons, only one lets God do the work he wants to do in us.

And pray for your child, whether your child thought herself disobedient, obedient, or in between. What does your child's answer say about her self-image? How can you help her celebrate the times she's obedient?

"ONE ACT OF OBEDIENCE IS BETTER THAN ONE HUNDRED SERMONS."

—Dietrich Bonhoeffer

Pray:

Dear God, it's strange thinking of how you came to earth and had to obey, just as we do. Yet you obeyed your Father out of love, not obligation. Help us obey in the same way, fueled by the same motive. Amen.

For All the Right Reasons

Objective: To practice obedience with people so we're better able to obey Jesus.

Jigsaw Puzzles

It's chart time!

Ask your Jigsaw Puzzle to think about what he or she will be asked to do at your house in the coming week, then to create a chart that lists those things. Rather than calling this a "chore chart," label it an "obedience chart."

The goal is for your Jigsaw Puzzle to own this process and see it as practice for obeying Jesus. Help your child brainstorm what are common requests (picking up clothing, cleaning a room, doing dishes, etc.). Avoid the temptation to "pile on" tasks; rather, look for your child to list what he or she recalls.

Superballs

Team up with your Superball to do a 120-Minute Obedience Marathon. Make a joint list of tasks that you've been asked to do and then pick a two-hour session in which you together attempt to accomplish as many of them as possible.

Painting a room is probably out, but cleaning...yard work... running errands...generate a list of small, ongoing tasks.

Plan for an exhausting time (you, not your Superball!) of obedience fun.

After the two-hour obedience binge, sit down with a treat and talk about how it felt to obey by choice. How otherwise boring tasks can be fun when you're anticipating how pleased the person who asked you to do them will be.

Teddy Bears

Together, select someone who normally has requests for one or both of you. It may be another parent, or a neighbor who needs help, or a teacher. Decide to honor every request this week—and to do your best to obey the person the same way you'd obey Jesus.

This will require ongoing communication (not a bad thing!) and some joint effort. If your child is asked to pick up his or her room, do it together. If you're asked to take out the trash, do it as a team.

You'll model obedience—and you'll have more time with your child. Plus, you'll make someone very happy!

SESSION 3

Making Good Choices

Disciples do what Jesus wants them to do...but how can your child know what Jesus wants? Here are ways your child can be sure to make good choices.

A note from Grant

Coke or Pepsi? Plastic or paper? Ah, if only it were always so easy!

Your child is just starting to make choices that can have life-changing consequences. For younger kids, many of their issues are black and white—obedience and disobedience; truth and dishonesty.

As kids become more independent, they deal with "the big stuff"...which friends to hang out with, what TV shows or movies to watch, what Web sites to visit, and what they'll wear.

And sooner or later you won't be around to help your child make good, God-pleasing decisions.

That's why you're going to equip your child with a few easy, memorable filters that provide guidance in making choices that honor God and deepen faith and trust in him. Kids who start using these guidelines now will develop the healthy habit of thinking through decisions they face.

The Point:

Disciples make choices that honor and obey Jesus.

What you'll need:

A quarter

A clean paper coffee filter

A coffee pot with old coffee grounds in the filter

Discipler Tip

A 20-minute walk is prime time to build relationship—it's just you and your child. Talk about some of the choices he or she may be facing in school, friendships, or activities. Listen intently and you'll discover a lot about your child!

Dive In

Heads or Tails? (20 minutes)

Before this activity, think of a place you and your child can easily walk to in about 10 minutes. It might be a local park, store, school, or landmark.

Grab a quarter and tell your child you're heading out for a walk. If the weather is bad, take your child for a drive instead, but follow the same guidelines. Stand in front of your house and hand your child the quarter.

Say: **We're going to walk to** (name the place you chose ahead of time)...**but we're taking a different route. Every time we come to a corner, flip the coin. If the coin turns up heads, we go right. Tails, we go left. Ready? Flip the quarter to start us off.**

Walk for ten minutes, following the directions "given" by the coin. You may not reach your intended destination—that's OK. Then turn around and walk back home.

As you walk home, talk about these questions:

- **How did the coin affect our trip to** (name your destination)?
- **Was this a good way to make decisions? Why or why not?**
- **What are some choices that kids your age are making?**

Say: **As a disciple of Jesus, your decisions should honor and obey Jesus. Let's talk some more about how to make good choices.**

Dig In

STOP Sign (20 minutes)

As you near your home, find a stop sign and stand near it with your child. Ask:

- **When cars come up to this sign, what are three things the driver might do?**
- **Are those good things to do? Why or why not?**

Say: **I'd be a bad driver if I stopped here, closed my eyes, then just kept going. Drivers need to look both ways to see if there's any traffic coming. They need to be aware of what's going on around them. They need to see other people around them and decide what's best to do.**

In life, we all need to stop sometimes to make good choices. As a follower of Jesus, our choices should honor and obey him. Let's head home and think some more about how to make good, God-pleasing decisions.

Go inside and sit down with your child. Gather a Bible, a sheet of paper, and a pen. With your child, brainstorm (and write down) three choices your child makes on a regular basis. For example, your child might write down "What TV shows to watch," "Which songs I'll listen to," and "How I treat kids at school."

Say: **I'm going to give you a cool tool to use every time you need to make a choice like these. Just remember the stop sign we saw. When it comes to making good choices...just STOP. S-T-O-P. Each letter reminds you of something to consider. Let's start with "S."**

If I do this, will I be *safe?* Help your child look up and read aloud Psalm 139:13-14. Talk about how your child's body was created by God, and is a precious gift to care for and treasure.

The next letter is "T." If I do this, will I be *truthful?* Sometimes you'll be tempted to make a choice that might lead you to lie—either now or in the future. Help your child look up and read aloud Proverbs 12:22. Briefly discuss why lying is something God hates.

Discipler Tip

As you talk about making good choices, don't be afraid to share a time when you had to make a hard decision or a time you made a bad choice. Being honest with our kids can help them see what happens when we've turned to God—or not turned to God.

"YOU HAVE BRAINS IN YOUR HEAD.
YOU HAVE FEET IN YOUR SHOES.
YOU CAN STEER YOURSELF
ANY DIRECTION YOU CHOOSE."

—Dr. Seuss (Theodor Geisel)

The next letter is "O." If I do this, will I be *obedient to my parents?* Help your child look up and read aloud Colossians 3:20. Talk about how parents have more wisdom and experience in life...plus they love their kids and want the best for them.

Finally, ask: **If I do this, will it be *pleasing to God?* That's the letter "P."** Guide your child in looking up and reading Ephesians 5:1. Talk about what it means to be an imitator of God—doing things that God would like.

Say: **If you answer "no" to any of these questions, it's probably a good idea to go in the other direction and make a better choice.**

Quickly review what the letters remind us to do. Remember, you're giving your child a tool to use, but not a test. Let your child use the examples he or she wrote down and practice using the STOP letters as a decision-making guideline.

Choices, Choices, Choices

Objective: To consider how obeying Jesus filters out some nasty consequences from our lives.

Jigsaw Puzzles

Help your child use a concordance to look up several verses about wisdom. You might consider Proverbs 3:5 or Ephesians 1:7. Let your child write out a few verses on the filter. Your child may want to use the filter as a bookmark or simply hang it in a prominent place in his or her room.

Superballs

With your child, gather leaves, grass, or pebbles and drop them into a glass of water. As you add the "junk" to the water, let your child share about some of the choices he or she might be facing in the coming week, month, or year. Hold the filter over an empty glass and let your child pour the dirty water over the filter.

Teddy Bears

Let your child drip dots of colored water onto the coffee filter. As the color spreads, blending with other colors, talk about how our choices influence those around us. Discuss specific family members or friends who are affected by the decisions your child makes each day.

Make It Mine

Say: **Stopping to make good choices allows you to filter out some bad stuff. Take a look at what I mean.**

Show your child the coffee grounds and used coffee filter. Ask:

- **How would you feel about seeing this sludgy stuff in your drink?**

Say: **The filter strained out all the coffee grounds. When you stop to make good, God-pleasing choices, you stop some nasty consequences from coming into your life.** Bring out a clean, unused paper coffee filter. **Let's use this coffee filter to make a handy reminder that disciples make choices that honor and obey Jesus.**

Choose an activity from the ones listed on the previous page. After the activity, pray with your child, asking God to help your child make choices that are pleasing to God.

"I keep asking that the God of our Lord Jesus Christ, the glorious Father, may give you the Spirit of wisdom and revelation, so that you may know him better."

—Ephesians 1:17

Blessed to be a Blessing

It's hard to see your children make poor choices. The consequences are painful for them and heartbreaking for you. If only you could spare them the pain...

But even in the midst of human foolishness, God can do incredible things.

The Bible is packed with people who made poor decisions—David, Abram, Martha—but God redeemed and loved them. God still used these men and women to do wonderful, amazing things for his kingdom.

How might God work in and through your child?

We want our kids to have the tools to make good decisions, not only to help them avoid pain, but to grow closer to God in the process. As kids make it a habit to look to their Heavenly Father, they'll grow in their faith. They'll discover what it means to hear God's voice. They'll learn to rely on God's wisdom.

"Wisdom outweighs any wealth."

—Sophocles

How does your child see *you* relying on God in the face of big decisions?

Have you humbly admitted making a poor choice?

How can God use one of your poor choices to bring about glory for his Kingdom?

Think about a poor choice your child has made recently. What prompted your child's misbehavior? How can knowing, loving, and following Jesus meet that need?

Pray:

Dear God, thank you for your mercy and forgiveness when we make bad choices. It must sadden you so much! Pour out godly wisdom into my child, so that he'll make choices that delight you, and glorify you. May his first thought be to look to his Heavenly Father for guidance. Amen.

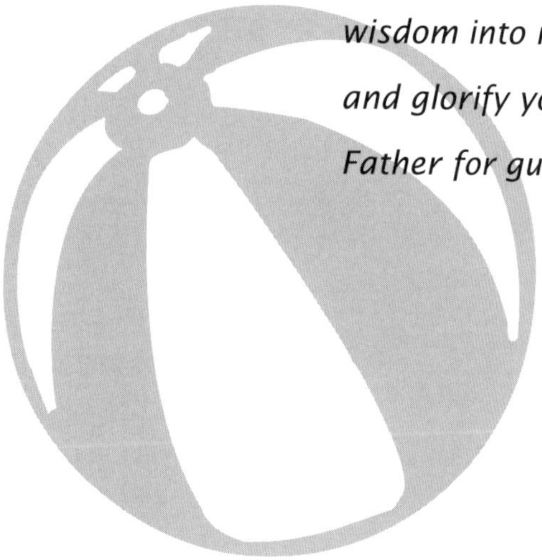

SESSION 4

Talking With Your Best Friend

Jesus loves talking with your child—and here's how your child can have great conversations with him.

A note from Grant

Most of the public prayer you hear in church and at the dinner table is so general in nature that we wouldn't notice if God answered the prayer. Think about it. When you ask God to bless you, how will you know if he does?

However, when you pray specifically, you're able to see God work—and know that he's active in the lives of his people.

I've noticed that God tends to answer prayers for new believers on a regular basis. It's as if he's looking for chances to give them what they need and desire. I think God has fun blessing his children—especially those who are new to the family. After all, he's a father who loves giving good gifts (Luke 11:5-13).

I've memorized Romans 8:32: "He who did not spare his own Son, but gave him up for us all—how will he not also, along with him, graciously give us all things?"

When it comes to prayer, asking isn't a burden or imposition on God. It's a signal that we're ready to receive what God has for us that fits within his will.

So why don't we ask?

The Point:

Jesus wants you to pray—and pray specifically,

What you'll need:

A Bible
Several flavors of ice cream
Your child's favorite ice cream toppings, such as chocolate sauce, nuts, or fruit
Items from your pantry or refrigerator, such as lettuce, salad dressing, broccoli, or fish
Bowls
Spoons
An inexpensive notebook
A pencil

Discipler Tip

While this lesson focuses most on *asking,* guide your child in applying the principle of specificity to *praising* God, too. For example, instead of praying, "Thank you, God, for the sunset," encourage your child to pray, "God, when I see that sunset I see how creative you are. Only you could come up with all those cool colors and paint them in the sky just like that. Wow—you're powerful and creative and I love you, God."

Dive In

Order Up! (10 minutes)

Set out a variety of flavors of ice cream, several of your child's favorite toppings, and a few "non-treats" such as pickles, salad dressing, broccoli, or fish. Be sure to peruse your shelves for items that would be truly disgusting if paired with ice cream. Hand your child a piece of paper (from the notebook) and a pencil.

Say: **I want to make you the best ice cream sundae on the planet. Look over the selection here, and then write down exactly what you want me to put in it.**

When your child has completed the ice cream "recipe," send him or her to another room. Then scoop up the tasty treat, following your child's order. Scoop up a sundae for yourself, then take the treats and join your child.

While you enjoy the ice cream, ask:

- **What was going through your mind while you were waiting in here?**
- **Did you trust me to give you what you'd asked for? Why or why not?**
- **How did you know that I gave you what you asked for?**
- **Say one word that describes how you felt when you looked into your bowl.**

Say: **I wanted to give you what you asked for, because I like when you feel** (if it's appropriate, say the word your child mentioned). **Prayer is a little like this. Jesus wants you to pray—and *pray specifically.* Let's explore that a little more.**

Dig In

A Loving, Heavenly Father (20 minutes)

Give your child the notebook and pencil.

Say: **Think for 15 seconds about all the things you've ever asked me for. It could have been at Christmas time or for a birthday, or any time.** After 15 seconds, continue: **Now, you've got one minute to make a list of everything you can think of. Go!**

Time your child for one minute, and then ask your child to read the list. As he reads the list, talk about the items you did give to your child.

Say: **I love you and I love giving you the things you ask for. The Bible has a passage that reminds me of that.** Help your child look up and read aloud Luke 11:5-10. Ask:

- **What does this passage tell you about God?**
- **What does this passage tell you about prayer?**

Say: **Let's keep reading.** Have your child read Luke 11:11-13. Repeat the above questions.

Tear out the sheet of paper your child just wrote on and set it aside to toss away later.

Say: **This book I've given you will be your very own prayer journal. You'll write specific prayer requests and praises in it every day—so keep it handy! You'll also write in your journal when God answers a prayer—that way you can see and remember how incredible God is.**

And when God answers "no," you may even be able to look back and understand why he said "no."

Jesus wants us to pray—and pray specifically. But that doesn't mean he's like a genie in a lamp or Santa Claus. These guidelines will help you pray specific, God-honoring prayers.

Help your child write the following guidelines on the inside cover of his or her prayer journal:

Baton Prayers

Add your prayers to those you've written on the prayer page in your baton. Once you've finished, return the prayer page to your baton.

"Expect great things from God. Attempt great things for God."

—William Carey

Is this request specific? How will I know when God answers the prayer? (Remember God can answer prayers "yes," "no," or "not now.")

Is this request selfish? Do I want God to give me something just because I like it, or because it might hurt someone I don't like?

Does this request match up with the Bible? Am I asking God for something he's clearly against?

Is this request wise? Would it really be a good idea for this to happen or for me to receive this?

Help your child write three prayer requests or praises, practicing making his or her prayers specific. You may want to choose one color of ink for requests, and another color of ink to write how God answered them. Encourage your child to keep the prayer journal handy, where he or she can keep track of prayers on a daily basis.

Practice Praying—Specifically!

Objective: To develop a habit of regular, specific prayer.

Jigsaw Puzzles

Help your child brainstorm specific topics he or she might reflect on during prayer time each day. For example, praying for your country, extended family members (by name), his or her school, or teachers. Let your child write one topic on a square of a calendar. Each day, your child can lift up specific prayers or praises about the topic for that day.

Superballs

Prayer doesn't just have to be done with bowed head and closed eyes! Help your child come up with five attributes of God. Go for a walk around your neighborhood and look for signs of those attributes. For example, you might see a huge old tree that reminds your child that God is mighty. Help your child lift up a prayer of praise, thanking God for that specific attribute.

Teddy Bears

Help your child send an e-mail or write a letter to friends and relatives, asking how he or she can pray for them specifically. If your child feels comfortable, he or she may want to call and ask personally.

As the responses come in, direct your child to write the requests or praises in the prayer journal. Then join with your child in praying for these specific things.

Make It Mine

(15 minutes)

Ask:

• **Why do you think it's important to record your prayers in a book like this?**

• **What do you think it'll be like to read this prayer journal in a year? What do you think you'll discover about God?**

Say: **Sometimes we forget that God answers our prayers in big ways. When you look back and see what God has done, you'll see the hand of your loving, Heavenly Father in your life.**

Jesus wants you to pray—and pray specifically. Let's practice that right now.

Choose an activity (previous page), and then pray for your child. Ask God to deepen your child's friendship with him through prayer.

Say: **After we finish today, I'm going to write in my prayer journal some specific prayers for your life. I'll add to my list of prayers in the next few weeks, then place that list in my baton** (available from Discipling Another to Love Jesus). **When we wrap up our discipling program I'll take out the list and show it to you.**

Be sure to actually do what you've promised—ask God for specific things to be in your child's life. Perhaps it's a godly wife or husband. A sense of calling. For a talent to blossom into something that effectively serves God. Be specific...and be long-winded. God wants to hear from you about your child!

Blessed to be a Blessing

We parents are probably some of the worst model pray-ers kids ever see. What parent hasn't rattled off a hurried, perfunctory prayer just to get the kids in bed, or to eat dinner while it's still hot?

Not exactly great modeling.

A GRANDFATHER WAS WALKING THROUGH HIS YARD WHEN HE HEARD HIS GRANDDAUGHTER REPEATING THE ALPHABET IN A TONE OF VOICE THAT SOUNDED LIKE A PRAYER. HE ASKED HER WHAT SHE WAS DOING. THE LITTLE GIRL EXPLAINED: "I'M PRAYING, BUT I CAN'T THINK OF EXACTLY THE RIGHT WORDS, SO I'M JUST SAYING ALL THE LETTERS, AND GOD WILL PUT THEM TOGETHER FOR ME, BECAUSE HE KNOWS WHAT I'M THINKING."

—Charles B. Vaughan

As you know, your child is watching...so take advantage of every moment. That doesn't mean your prayers need to be long-winded or use King James English. Keep your prayers short, sweet, and specific. And when God answers...celebrate big!

What specific things are you praying for your child?

How has God answered your prayers for your child? How have you thanked God?

Have you shared God's answers with your child?

How has God answered your child's prayers?

Pray:

Dear God, I want eyes that see what you're doing in and around me. I want to cooperate with your purposes. Teach me to pray specifically—and then to faithfully obey you when you make clear your will. You're a good God—no matter how you answer my prayers. Amen.

SESSION 5

Letters From a Friend

If a friend wrote your child a letter, that letter would be read. The Bible is a letter from Jesus! Here's how to dive into the Bible.

A note from Grant

If you were doing a report on Bolivia, would you grab the encyclopedia and begin at the beginning?

No.

You don't really care about the wonderful peculiarities of aardvarks. You're not interested in the charms of an abomasums (fourth stomach chamber of a ruminant—look it up).

Unless aardvarks and abomasums are Bolivia's chief exports, they're of zero interest. You need information about Bolivia.

The same is true for introducing new believers to the Bible. They're most interested in passages that are relevant. That answer questions they're asking. That speak to them where they are.

It's essential that new believers—children included—engage in Bible study. Otherwise, they don't benefit from guidance the Bible provides. When they memorize key passages, they're more protected in times of temptation.

As you disciple your child, encourage him to memorize specific passages. Those specific, key "Life Verses" are like armor, guarding a child's heart and mind today and for years to come.

We'll suggest some life verses that address specific issues in new believers' lives. Please take seriously the need to help your child learn these verses as you learn them (yup: you'll model this!), and to not only learn the words but to let the truth sink deeply into your minds and hearts.

The Point:

Disciples must know—and live out—Bible truth...starting with the fundamentals.

What you'll need:

A kickable ball
A trashcan lid or other large, flat, solid item to use as a shield
Bible
A pen
Your child's Prayer Notebook

Dive In

One-Armed Goalie (15 minutes)

Meet your child outside with a soccer ball or other "kickable" ball. Determine what will be your goal and station your child in front of it. Your goal might be "that fence" or "between those trees." It needn't be anything elaborate.

Be sure the size of the goal is in proportion to your child's age and ability. For example, if your child is small, make a smaller goal so he or she can protect it.

Say: **You're the goalie and I'm going to take some shots at your goal. Let's see how well you can keep the ball out of the goal. Ready? Oh, wait...I almost forgot. Raise the hand that you write with. Now put that hand behind your back. You can't move it or use it at all. Ready?**

Back up a bit and take a few shots at the goal, always aiming for the side where your child is least protected—the arm that's behind his or her back. After a few minutes, stop and ask:

- **What word best describes how that felt?**

Say: **It looks like you need some help on that side.**

Hand your child the trashcan lid. She can hold it any way she wishes, and use it to help protect the goal. Play again, continuing to aim for the weaker side. Your child should find it easier to defend the goal.

After a few minutes, take the ball and give your child a high-five... and maybe a drink of cold water! Ask:

- **What was the difference between the first part of the game and the second part?**
- **Why do you think I aimed for your right (or left) side every time?**

Discipler Tip

In the days and weeks leading up to this session, prayerfully consider what Life Issues your child wrestles with. It may be honesty, doubt, selfishness, or anger. Take the time to think and pray about what you've seen, heard, and generally observed in your child. You know your child pretty well, but God knows him even better!

• How did you feel when you had a shield to help you?

Say: **As you grow in your friendship with God, there's someone who'd like for you *not* to grow closer to God. That's Satan. He's God's enemy and spends a lot of his time trying to find ways to keep us from becoming better friends with God.**

Just like I always shot for your weak side, Satan wants to find where you're the weakest and use those weaknesses to pull you away from God.

Fortunately, God's given you a shield—the Bible. That's why disciples must know—and live out—Bible truth...starting with the basics. So what are those basics?

Dig In

Life Issues, Life Verses (20 minutes)

Say: **The Bible—God's Word—is awesome, life-changing, and important. It's also *huge!* Sometimes you might feel like it's too hard to find the stuff in here that's most important to you.**

So first let's think about what issues or topics are important to you. Think quietly while I read some questions. You may want to write some of your thoughts in your prayer notebook. No one needs to see them except you.

• **What are one or two areas of weakness that Satan might find in your life?**

• **When do you feel like you've let God down, or aren't doing what he wants you to do?**

• **Complete this sentence: When I think about meeting Jesus face-to-face, I wish he wouldn't know that I...**

• **I don't feel close to God when I...**

Say: **Now, tear up that paper and throw it away. Think about some of the things you wrote down. They probably mostly fall into one of these three areas of weakness:**

Discipler Tip

Ideally, you should play this game outside as a way to engage a child's whole body. However, if you don't have a playing area or the weather is bad, you can play at the dining room table using a ping pong ball or even a folded paper "football."

Discipler Tip

If your child isn't familiar with his or her Bible, take five minutes to give a quick "crash course" in the basics of using a Bible. Point out the books of the Bible in the table of contents, and then explain that each book has chapters and verses (large numbers and small numbers).

Discipler Tip

If your child struggles to identify a Life Issue, offer a suggestion or two. Remember to be supportive and positive, rather than critical, as you share what you've observed. Have your child write down one or two Life Issues.

- **wanting to please yourself**
- **wanting the sinful things you see**
- **being too proud of what you have (and who you are)**

Say: **We'll call these things Life Issues, and everyone has at least one! The good thing is that God has given us a letter—the Bible—filled with encouragement and wisdom to strengthen us when we face our Life Issues.**

Let's look together to see what encouragement God has for you.

Use the list of verses related to some common Life Issues on page 105 to guide your child in looking up and reading some verses in his or her Bible. Select short, easy-to-remember passages that will be meaningful and helpful to your child. You may need to look up several verses to find ones that really "click" with your child.

Let your child write out each Scripture passage in his or her Prayer Notebook.

Ask:

- **Think of a specific time when this passage could help you keep from sinning.**
- **How will knowing these verses deepen your friendship with God?**

Say: **I'm so glad God's given us help in the Bible! Jesus wants his disciples to know—and live out—Bible truth, starting with the basics. Now that you know some basics, let's see what it means to live them out.**

Make It Mine

(10 minutes)

Say: **God won't leave you hanging—he's giving you a shield. But you have to pick it up and use it! That takes some effort. Let me show you what I mean by giving you a quick quiz:**

1. What's your phone number?

2. What's your address?

3. What's your birthday?

Say: **Wow! 100%! Ask:**

- **How did you know all those things?**
- **Why did you memorize them?**

Say: **We memorize things that help us or things that we use all the time. That's why you need to memorize these verses you wrote down. Every day, you'll remember them—kind of like a soldier putting on armor.**

Choose one of the activities on the following page. After the activity, pray with your child, asking God to make his Word come alive in your child's life each day.

Blessed to be a Blessing

Many of us remember memorizing Scriptures to receive a gold star or piece of candy. If that's how we learned, it's likely we remember the prize more than what we memorized!

When we "bribe" children to memorize Scripture, we're communicating that it's a chore...that it's not important enough to do for its own sake.

Instead of offering a bribe, elevate God's Word so your child appreciates that it's a treasure—something to be held close. The Bible has the power to transform our children's hearts and minds, and to draw

"THE BIBLE IS GOD'S CHART FOR YOU TO STEER BY, TO KEEP YOU FROM THE BOTTOM OF THE SEA, AND TO SHOW YOU WHERE THE HARBOR IS, AND HOW TO REACH IT WITHOUT RUNNING ON ROCKS OR BARS."

—Henry Ward Beecher

them closer to God on a daily basis.

> "THE HOLY SCRIPTURES ARE OUR LETTER FROM HOME."
> —Augustine

Pray about the issues that you see your child struggling with. If you find a helpful or applicable Scripture, write it on a note card and place it where you child will see it.

What Life Issues do you see your child struggling with?

What Scriptures do you think would be most meaningful and transforming to your child?

Using God's Word

Objective: To learn both the words and meaning of specific Bible passages.

Jigsaw Puzzles

Allow your child to spend time reflecting on the passages. Then direct him or her to write one passage in his or her own words in the Prayer Notebook.

Say: **Now write three situations when it will be helpful to remember this verse. After you write each situation, say the verse aloud. Imagine how you'll feel when you say that verse in one of those situations!**

Superballs

Help your child come up with physical cues that will prompt him or her to say the verse each day. For example, "I'll read or recite the verse in my head every time I brush my teeth." Or, "I'll read this passage when I pour my cereal each morning."

Then help your child tape notecards with the verses written on them near the place that action takes place (for example, on the bathroom mirror or on the cereal box). Rather than just slapping the notecard on the fridge, put it on the milk container or on something that your child will touch or use every day.

Being specific and unique will help your child see and memorize the passages!

Teddy Bears

Commit to memorizing Scripture verses together.

Start by saying the first half of the verse, then directing your child to saying the second half. Then switch roles. Or put the Bible words to a melody that you both know. Plan to sing the Scripture together before bedtime or on the way to school.

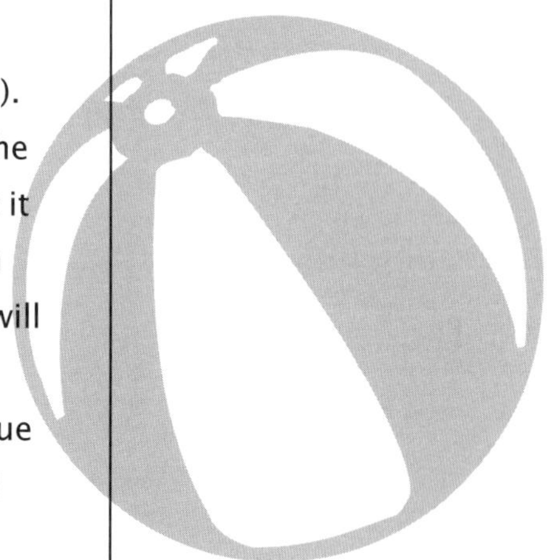

How can you encourage your child to continually seek guidance in the Bible?

Pray:

Dear God, thank you for the wisdom and guidance in the Bible. I pray that you place these specific passages into (child's name)'s heart...daily. I pray that your Word would guide him through life, and deepen his love for you. Amen.

SESSION 6

Fun, Friends, and Fellowship

We're in this disciple thing together! Here's how your child can find people to help him or her follow Jesus.

A note from Grant

So far you've been building new—and sometimes challenging—skills into your kids. Scripture memory and prayer require kids to develop a new set of "muscles."

But fellowship is a natural for most kids. Kids like spending time with friends, they're pretty good at making new friends, and churches tend to provide ample opportunities for kids to plug into.

So why do we need to focus on fellowship?

While kids may think hanging out with their friends from church is a no-brainer, it's still a vital aspect of faith development...one you want your child to practice into adulthood. This session will also allow you to raise the bar when it comes to defining fellowship.

You'll help your child discover that fellowship means more than hanging out with a buddy. And there's a greater benefit than simply having someone to take the other side in a game of HORSE or a "Destructo Master Marauder" video game tournament. Show your child that Christian friendships also strengthen our friendship with Jesus.

The Point:

Disciples live out their faith together—encouraging each other.

What you'll need:

A Bible
A box of toothpicks
4 yards of inexpensive yarn
Scissors

Discipler Tip

This session is a good reminder to find places where your child can develop quality, lifelong Christian friendships. Take a look at the opportunities you're giving your child to build these critical relationships.

Dive In

Pick-Up Picks (15 minutes)

Sit on the floor with your child. Take all the toothpicks from the box and hold them in your fist.

Say: **We're going to play a game. We both start with five points. I'll drop these toothpicks on the floor and we'll take turns picking them up one at a time. Sounds easy enough, right? Well, maybe.**

If you move a toothpick *other* than the one you're touching, you lose a point. Let's see if either of us can finish with any points. Ready?

Hold your hand an inch or so above the ground and drop the toothpicks. Ideally, you want some to fall away from the bunch, but most of them will be touching. Play until all the toothpicks are picked up, or until you're both out of points. Then ask:

- **Which toothpicks did you try to get first? Why?**
- **Why was it harder to get the toothpicks that were together?**

Say: **The toothpicks that were sticking near their toothpick buddies lasted a lot longer than the ones off on their own. Ask:**

- **Why do you think it's important for Christians to stick close to other Christians?**

Say: **Today we're talking about something called "fellowship." That's kind of a fancy word for spending time with other people. God wants his followers to hang out together, to be friends, to encourage each other, and to love each other. Let's see what the Bible has to say about fellowship.**

Dig In

Intertwined (20 minutes)

Hold up one yard of yarn.

Say: **First, let's pretend this is a Christian…like you or me. In fact, we'll call this guy "Christian." Christian wants to follow God and do the things that please God. Hold one end of Christian to represent Christian following God.**

Hand your child one end of the yarn.

But sometimes, Christian is tempted to do wrong things—to sin.

Hold the other end of the yarn.

Say: **I'll hold this end to represent Christian's other friends. You see, some of his friends aren't Jesus-followers. They're pretty OK even though they sometimes lie, cheat now and then, and gossip on the bus ride home from school.**

So sometimes Christian hangs out with them and…well, he's pulled right along with the things they do.

Pull on the string, gradually increasing the strength with which you pull.

He figures it's OK—I mean lots of other people do those things, right? And all that stuff he's learned…well, it's just for church, right?

Pull until your child loses his or her grip, or the yarn breaks. Ask:

- **Uh-oh. What happened to Christian?**
- **What would have helped Christian?**

Say: **There's a verse that talks about this.** Help your child look up and read aloud Ecclesiastes 4:9-12. Ask:

- **How does this verse remind you of Christian?**
- **What do you think this verse means?**

Say: **God knows we need friends who'll help us follow and obey him. That's fellowship. We're going to create a cord of three strands, just like the one mentioned in the verse you just read.**

Lay one new piece of yarn on the floor. Have your child look up and read aloud Proverbs 27:17.

Say: **This verse talks about "sharpening" another person. An axe isn't very good if it isn't sharp. So when we talk about**

sharpening someone, we're talking about helping someone use their gifts to serve God.

This cord we just laid down will represent someone who gives you chances to use your gifts to serve God. Have your child touch the yarn and say the name of a friend or relative who encourages him or her to serve God.

Lay down another length of yarn on top of the first one. Then help your child look up and read aloud 1 John 3:16. Ask:

- **Think of someone who has given something up for you. Someone who would do anything for you...just because they love you.** Pause. Ask:
- **How does that person help you follow Jesus?**

Say: **Say that person's name while you touch the second cord.**

Discipler Tip

Some kids may have trouble coming up with three solid, Christian friends or relatives. That's OK. Use that opportunity as a time to pray specifically for God to provide a group of close, Christian friends.

Lay down another length of yarn on top of the other two. Help your child look up and read aloud Proverbs 27:6. Ask:

- **Why would a friend want to wound or hurt you?**

Say: **This isn't about getting in a fist fight with your best friend. God wants us to have friends who don't mind telling us the truth...even if it means hurting our feelings. God knows those are friends who love you enough to help you make good choices. Think of a friend whose feelings you'd risk hurting, if it meant keeping that friend from doing something wrong.**

Say that person's name while you touch the third cord.

Take the three pieces of yarn and knot them together, about four inches from each end. Hand one end to your child and stand facing each other, so the cord is taut between you (but not too tight). Each of you should begin twisting your end of the rope, to the right. Soon the rope will begin to "crimp" in the middle. When it does, reach into the center of the rope, and pull the middle straight down. Bring the ends (with the knots) together. You've just made a short length of very sturdy rope!

Tie a knot in each end of the rope and let your child pull on the rope. Ask:

• **What's the difference between this rope and the first piece of string we used?**

• **How can Christian friends make a difference in your friendship with Jesus?**

Make It Mine

(10 minutes)

Say: **God wants you to have close, Christian friends so you can be strong when you're tempted to do wrong things. But there's another reason.** Help your child look up and read aloud 1 Corinthians 12:14-20. Ask:

• **How is the family of God like a body?**

• **What do you think God wants you to learn from this passage?**

Say: **We all have special gifts and abilities. When we work together—like a body—we can do amazing things for God. That's another reason why God wants us to have special friendships with other Christians—so we can work together and do the work God has for us.**

Choose one of the activities on page 57. After the activity, pray with your child, asking God to give your child relationships that will provide fellowship.

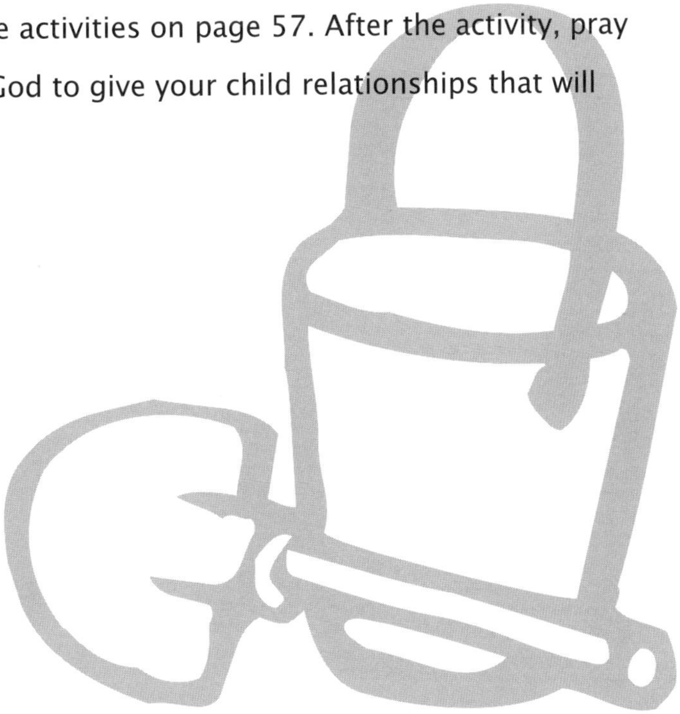

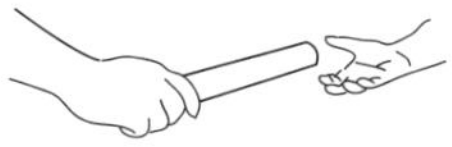

Baton Prayers

Add your prayers for your child's relationships to those prayers you've written on the prayer page in your baton. Once you've finished, return the prayer page to your baton.

"A JUDICIOUS FRIEND, INTO WHOSE HEART WE MAY POUR OUT OUR SOULS, AND TELL OUR CORRUPTIONS AS WELL AS OUR COMFORTS, IS A VERY GREAT PRIVILEGE."

—George Whitefield

> "For the early Christians, koinonia was not the frilly 'fellowship' of church-sponsored bi-weekly outings. It was not tea, biscuits, and sophisticated small talk in the Fellowship Hall after the sermon. It was an unconditional sharing of their lives with the other members of Christ's body."
>
> —Ron Sider

Blessed to be a Blessing

There's a delicate balance between allowing our kids to be a Christian witness to non-Christians and surrounding them with a supportive, encouraging blanket of Christ-followers. Be sure they've got the blanket of Christian relationships before you send them out as a light. Find opportunities to nurture and feed your child's friendships with other Christian kids.

Does your child have one friend who would keep him or her accountable in a tough situation?

If you could design the perfect friend for your child, what traits would that person have?

What opportunities are you giving your child to develop meaningful Christian friendships?

What sort of friend is your child to other Christian kids?

Pray:

Dear God, thank you for the support and encouragement that comes when we knit our hearts with other followers. Lead my child to friends who will guide her closer to you. Help my child seek out other kids who hold her values and passion for you. Knit their hearts together and help them strengthen each other. Amen.

Finding Friends and Fellowship

Objective: To become intentional about pursuing fellowship relationships.

Jigsaw Puzzles

Help your child think and journal about his or her gifts and abilities.

Here's an easy way: make a list of five things you love to do. For each item listed, write a way that might help someone in the church. Then read 1 Corinthians 12:27-31 together. Look over the list and consider what gifts God might want your child to use to serve him.

Superballs

Cut out 1-inch by 6-inch strips of paper. On each paper, write the name of a friend or relative. Turn over each piece of paper and write down a special gift or ability that person has. Let your child use the paper strips to make a paper chain to keep in a prominent place. Encourage your child to add to the paper chain as he or she develops new friendships.

Teddy Bears

Help your child think of three close friends—perhaps ones that were mentioned in the "Dig In" activity. Guide your child in planning a special get-together for each of these friends. Think about their likes, dislikes, and what activities might mean the most to each individual.

Remember, you don't need to spend additional dollars—most kids are happy just to spend time together, deepening their friendships.

Be sure you follow through—give your child the opportunity to spend special time with his close friends.

SESSION 7

Sharing Your Story

Jesus wants you and your child to share what he's doing in your life with friends. How? By sharing your story. You'll discover how!

A note from Grant

It may be hard to imagine your elementary-aged child has enough life experience to have a story to tell. It's like seeing that an actor has published his memoirs—and he's 24 years old.

But here's the reality of God working in our lives: God brings about change. That's true in adults...and true in children. Including your child.

Your child's faith story is simply describing that change. What might seem like a small change to you—becoming comfortable at school, or no longer being afraid of change—can be a very big deal to your child. Don't underestimate the power of your child's story when shared with others!

A faith story includes three pieces: who Jesus is, what Jesus has done, and what that's meant in your child's life. It's that simple...and that powerful.

When your child begins sharing his faith story, two things happen:

First, he identifies himself as a Christian. That's a powerful step in walking as a disciple.

And second, he'll see God open up opportunities to share his story with others. God will use him to touch others. To speak on Jesus' behalf at school, at home, in friendships. His faith will deepen as he sees God work.

Keep in mind that a faith story is a *simple* story. Encourage your child to craft and rehearse a story that's accurate, just a few sentences long, and easy to present.

By the way, this is an excellent time for you to craft your own faith story, to share as a model for your child.

The Point:

Disciples share their faith stories with others.

What you'll need:

A map of your city or town
Pencils
Your Prayer Notebooks
Two Bibles

Dive In

Can You Hear Me? (20 minutes)

Say: **We use telephones to talk to people far away. Imagine trying to talk to someone across the ocean without the help of a phone...you could yell as loud as possible and still not be heard.**

Get out the map and set it in front of your child. Locate your home on the map.

Say: **Let's try an experiment. Suppose you've got some good news to share with** (name of a friend who lives at least a mile away). **The good news: you won a prize from an electronics store. You and a friend can go in and pick out whatever you can carry—games, cell phones, computers, anything. And you're going to take** (name of friend) **with you.**

Let's see if you can get your friend's attention by yelling. Yell out the good news and tell your friend to call right away. Give it a try.

Pause after your child yells.

Say: **Odd...no call from your friend. Either your good news wasn't good enough, or the message didn't go through.**

Maybe you were facing the wrong direction. Consult the map. **Let's figure out which way to aim your voice and try again. Ready? Yell!**

Pause.

Say: **Still nothing. Wow...maybe I should help. Being a parent, I have a lot of practice yelling, you know. Together let's yell,** "(friend's name), **call** (your child's name) **right away to get free, cool stuff!"**

Pause.

Say: **You know, it doesn't matter how good your news is if nobody hears it.**

Discuss the following with your child:

- **What would have helped your message connect with your friend?**

- **How would your friend feel if you gave up now and took someone else to the electronics store for free stuff?**
- **When someone wants you to understand a message, what helps you receive the message clearly?**

Say: **Jesus does a great job giving us a message in Matthew, chapter 28. He's clear, he keeps the message simple, and he delivers it in person to his disciples—who are told to pass it along.**

That means as Jesus' disciples now, this message is for *us*, too. Let's read it.

Read Matthew 28:19-20 aloud. If your child is able, ask your child to read the passage.

With your child, discuss:

- **What is Jesus asking us disciples to do in this passage?**
- **What are three ways we might do what he asks?**

Say: **Telling people about Jesus is like sharing good news with a friend: we have to be close enough so the friend can hear us. And we have to share the message in a way that makes sense to our friend. It helps if we're clear, too.**

Let's figure out how we might share the good news about Jesus. We'll practice together, so we're ready when Jesus wants us to share his good news.

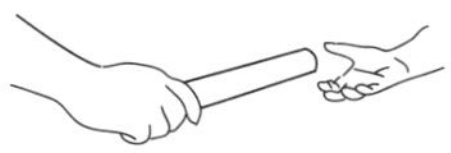

Baton Prayers

Add your prayers for your child's ability to be faithful in reflecting Jesus' values in a culture that often fails to do the same. Once you've finished, return the prayer page to your baton.

Dig In

Your Faith Story

Say: **When we share our faith story—the story of what Jesus has done for us—it's important that we keep our message clear and simple. When we try to give too much information to someone, things get confusing.**

Here's an example.

Discipler Tip

Editing down your faith stories to what's most important is tougher than it looks. It may take you a few tries to wordsmith your faith stories. Don't do the work for your child; encourage, nudge, clarify with questions, but let your child decide how to formulate the first section for both of you. The second and third sections must be done individually; your answers won't be the same.

Suppose you asked me if I had a favorite song and I said the following:

"Yes, I do. It's 'With a Little Help From My Friends' by the Beatles. Lennon and McCartney wrote the song and Ringo Starr sang it on the *Sgt. Pepper's Lonely Hearts Club Band* album, which was released on June 3, 1967, in the United States.

"The Beatles started recording the song on March 30, 1967, and finished it at 7:30 the next morning at the Abbey Road Studio in London.

"The song was ranked #304 on Rolling Stone magazine's list of the '500 Greatest Songs of All Time.' It has been number-one on the British singles charts three times, in 1968, 1988, and 2004."

All you wanted was a simple answer and I flooded you with facts.

That happens when we try to tell people about Jesus, too. There's so much to tell that we try to get it all in—and people quit listening.

So let's see if we can keep our faith stories short, clear, and personal.

Say: **Jesus wants you to tell your friends what he's doing in your life. How? By sharing your "faith story." Let's discover how!**

Our faith stories have three parts:

- **Who Jesus is,**
- **What we were like before we knew Jesus, and**
- **How Jesus has changed our lives.**

Say: **Everything else—Moses and the 10 Commandments, Jonah in the Belly of a Huge Fish, the parables Jesus told—can wait. They're good to know, but not the most important thing to share with someone who doesn't know Jesus.**

This is going to feel a bit like homework, but it's homework we'll do together. I need to sort out my faith story, too.

Both you and your child will need your Prayer Notebooks and a pencil with a substantial eraser; you'll both be writing and editing your individual faith stories.

Say: **At the top of your page write, "Jesus is..." In the center of the page write, "Before I met Jesus I was..." And toward the bottom of your page write "Because of Jesus..."**

Now we'll fill in the blanks. And our goal is to be able to read our faith stories aloud in less than 30 seconds!

Say: **The first section explains who Jesus is. If a friend asked you who Jesus is, how would you answer?**

Write down your child's answer, then work together to tighten and simplify the answer until it's only one or two brief sentences.

Say: **Next your paper says, "Before I met Jesus I was..." Write how you were before you knew Jesus. Maybe you were afraid of dying, or the dark. Maybe you felt guilty about the things you've done.**

After you and your child have answered, work together to tighten and simplify your answers.

Say: **Now it's time to share what Jesus has done in our lives. Let's be specific. If you were afraid of dying, or of the dark, now that you know Jesus, maybe you aren't afraid anymore. If you used to feel guilty about things you've done, maybe now you feel forgiven.**

After you and your child have answered, work together to tighten and simplify your answers.

Next, copy your answers onto clean sheets of paper and take turns reading your faith stories to each other. Use a watch to time yourselves; the goal is to comfortably, easily share your faith stories in less than 30 seconds each.

Here are some faith stories to help you see how yours might look:

Jesus is God's Son, and he's my forever friend. Before I met Jesus I felt alone. Now I know I'm loved and I never feel lonely.

Jesus is God's Son, and he came to earth because he loves us. Before I knew Jesus I was sad a lot, because my parents split up. Now I know that even when things are hard in my life I've got a friend who loves me and helps me feel better.

Make It Mine

Sharing Your Story

Say: **This week let's enjoy the adventure of sharing our faith stories with others.**

Discuss with your child:

- **Who is someone who might want to hear your faith story? Who cares about you or who wonders what makes you tick?**

It's tempting to pick someone who knows nothing about God—but as your child begins sharing her story, what matters is that she actually does it. It's fine to share her faith story with other Christians, too—it's an encouragement.

Begin with people who are likely to be receptive...you'll build your child's confidence.

And identify someone with whom you can share your story as well.

Blessed to be a Blessing

"WHILE YOU LIVE, TELL TRUTH AND SHAME THE DEVIL!"

—William Shakespeare

There's a new "virtue" shaping contemporary culture: tolerance. The notion that all belief systems and opinions are equally valid, are equally true.

While this belief is wonderful for avoiding conflict and encouraging political correctness, it places your child in a tough spot: is sharing his or her faith story with another person an act of intolerance? Is it implying that a faith in Jesus is more true than another belief system? And if that's the case, is it wrong to force a Christian perspective on others?

This "virtue" stands in stark opposition to the Gospel.

Yes, it's good to be tolerant and accepting. Jesus modeled both attributes endless times—but he never stepped away from proclaiming the truth, too. He could love a sinner and hate sin at the same time.

Probe how deeply "tolerance training" has impacted your child's world view. Does she understand that sharing her story is just that: sharing her story? That she has every right to share what Jesus has done and is doing for her? That stating a personal position isn't an imposition; it's an invitation to enter into dialogue?

Give your child permission to share her faith story by letting her see you share yours.

- What do you expect will be most challenging for your child in sharing her faith story?

"NOTHING IS AS FRUSTRATING AS ARGUING WITH SOMEONE WHO KNOWS WHAT HE'S TALKING ABOUT."

—Sam Ewig

Have I Got a Story for *You*

Objective: To share your faith story with a friend or family member.

Jigsaw Puzzles

Ask your child to carefully think through and write out his testimony, just the way he'd like to share it. Ask your child to pick a family member or friend who lives far away and post the testimony along with a cover letter explaining it's a message he'd like to share. Every word in the right place, everything evenly spaced, aesthetically pleasing...your Jigsaw will love it!

Superballs

Organize a hang-out time for your child and a friend of choice.

Ask your child to find a time during the hang-out time to talk about the discipling you're doing, and to share his or her faith story.

Your Superball will discover that it's okay to share a faith story while in the normal flow of a relationship, while having fun with a friend. Sharing one's faith doesn't need to be somber or formal—it happens best in the context of relationship.

Teddy Bears

Ask your child to share his or her faith story with a supportive family member or friend from church—someone who'll be especially receptive to the faith story. After sharing the faith story, encourage a dialogue about how sharing the faith story felt...how it might go the next time...and provide a warm encouragement for your sometimes sensitive child.

Then give your teddy bear a hug and pray together for other opportunities to share the faith story as God directs.

- How can you encourage your child this week?
- How open are you to sharing your faith story? What obstacles might be in your way?

Pray:

Dear God, I know you expect your followers to be bold in declaring their allegiance to you, that you say those who confess you will have the favor returned when you do the same for us in Heaven. Give both my child and me boldness, God—and opportunity this week to go public with our faith. Amen.

SESSION 8

Staying Strong

Disciples sometimes start out following Jesus and then wander off to follow other things. You and your child will learn how to stay strong!

A note from Grant

Healthy and strong.

We want those words to describe our children the moment they're born...and all their lives.

Healthy and strong. Physically...emotionally...mentally...and spiritually.

We carefully watch out for the health and strength of our children in some ways—we provide healthy food and help with homework. Unfortunately, some parents are less intentional about tending to the spiritual health and strength of their children. They delegate spiritual development to the Christian Education department of their churches.... which is good—but there's something better.

You're better.

As your child's discipler, you're bucking that trend. You're investing in the spiritual life of your child in a powerful way. You've stepped up to the plate of being the primary faith-shaper in your child's life.

And we bless you for it.

Strong, healthy disciples grow in their willingness and ability to follow Jesus. Which means as your child grows in the faith, your child will join you on the journey of discipleship. A journey made stronger by...

- Spending time in prayer
- Building and growing relationships with other believers
- Spending time studying the Bible
- Sharing your faith story

The Point:

Disciples grow stronger in loving Jesus and steadily better at following him.

What you'll need:

No supplies needed

Dive In

Strong Arms (20 minutes)

Say: **Here's a challenge for you: hold your arms out to the side, even with your shoulders, until I tell you to put them down.**

While you hold that position, I'll tell you about someone who found himself in a similar position.

First, let me tell you how strong you look doing that. It's quite impressive.

Moses was leading the Israelites out of Egypt when they ran into conflict. God promised to give the Israelites victory in a battle with a people called the Amalekites, so God's people went out to fight.

However, God said his promise was only good so long as Moses held his staff over his head. If he lowered his hands the Amalekites would start winning and the Israelites would start losing.

How are your arms feeling, by the way? Tired? Aching yet?

Moses had to hold his arms up for an entire day! While holding a wooden staff! About now you're seeing just how hard that would be, right?

But God gave Moses two helpers—Aaron and Hur. They had Moses sit on a rock, and sitting down helped a little. They then helped a lot by helping Moses hold his arms up. Without the help of Aaron and Hur, Moses never would have made it and the Israelites would have lost. But with their help, the battle was won.

Let me give you a little help, here.

Come stand facing me and put your arms on my shoulders.

Isn't that easier? Holding all that weight alone is really hard, but when you have someone to help keep you strong, it makes everything possible.

Go ahead and shake out your arms and have a seat.

Pause while your child tells you how much that hurt! Then continue.

Say: **This event in Moses' life is a great example of why God wants us to be in relationship with other Christians—we aren't strong enough to make it through the hard times of life alone.**

Read Exodus 17:8-13 aloud. If your child is able, ask your child to read the passage.

With your child, discuss:

- **Why do you think God didn't make us strong enough to do everything on our own?**
- **Describe a time you helped someone do something they couldn't do by themselves. How did that feel?**

Say: **We need to ask others for help when we're hurting. And we need to help others who need us.**

Now please help me clean the house, do the laundry, fix dinner, and wash the dishes.

Just kidding...maybe.

Dig In

Four Limbs Are Better Than One!

Say: **We've been practicing four habits that help disciples stay strong in our friendship with Jesus:**

- **Spending time in prayer**
- **Building and growing relationships with other believers**
- **Spending time studying the Bible**
- **Sharing your faith story**

But are they really that important? Couldn't we just do two or three of them and still be okay?

Please get on your hands and knees. We'll do an experiment and then decide if we really need to have all four disciplines in our lives.

After your child is on all fours say: **You have four parts of you on the floor right now: your right hand, your left hand, your right leg, and your left leg. If I try to push you over, it's going to be easy for you to stay strong and steady.**

Give your child a firm but gentle push.

Say: **See? You're staying strong. But let's say we take your left hand off the ground.**

Push your child again, gently but firmly.

Say: **Was it as easy to stay upright? Probably not.**

Let's take your right leg off the ground.

Push your child again.

Say: **Easier? Harder? You look a little shaky. Now let's take your left leg off the ground. How's that working for you?**

Help your child up and say: **That last one *really* made you unstable!**

Ask:

- **At what point in our experiment did you start to feel less stable, less strong?**
- **If I offered you $100 to get in your strongest position, which of the four positions would you pick: four on the floor, three on the floor, two on the floor, or one on the floor? Why?**

Say: **You can forget the $100 from me, but Jesus offers you an even better deal. Here's what James writes: "Blessed is the man who perseveres under trial, because when he has stood the test, he will receive the crown of life that God has promised to those who love him."** (James 1:12)

The four habits—prayer, fellowship, Bible study, and sharing our faith story—help us grow in our relationship with Jesus. And what we get is a great, adventurous life now and life in Heaven forever!

So let's stay strong. It's worth it!

Read 1 Corinthians 15:58 aloud. If your child is able, have your child read the verse.

Discuss:

- **What do you think it means to "give yourself fully to the work of the Lord"?**
- **The verse says to "let nothing move you." What do you think might be trying to move us?**

Say: **My goal for you—and Jesus' goal for you—is that you grow as a disciple. That you grow stronger in loving Jesus, and become ever better at following him.**

Baton Prayers

Add your prayers for your child's standing strong to those prayers you've written on the prayer page in your baton. Once you've finished, return the prayer page to your baton.

Make It Mine

Daily Workout

Say: **This week we'll practice staying strong. Every day let's spend time praying, reading the Bible, building our friendships with other Christians, and sharing our faith stories with each other—or other people.**

Agree on a daily time you'll tackle the four habits together, a time that fits both your schedules. Traveling on business? Do it by phone. Need to cancel another meeting? Do it—how seriously you take this week's tasks will communicate to your child how important the four habits are.

Discuss with your child:

- **Which of the four habits that keep us strong as disciples do you find hardest to do?**
- **How can I help you with that this week?**

"THE ONLY WAY TO REMAIN STRONG IS TO PRAY FOR OTHERS."
—Kuan Yin

Blessed to be a Blessing

The wisdom of staying spiritually strong is not reserved just for your child. We all struggle to remain on the path that God has laid out for us.

The priority you place on your spiritual strength training will be reflected in the life of your child. How seriously you take the daily

Strength Training

Objective: To start off the lifelong project of continuing to get stronger in our faith and where God is calling us.

Jigsaw Puzzles

Help your child make a checklist for the coming week. Decide together—with your Jigsaw taking the lead—how together you'll do Bible study, with whom you'll share your faith stories, how you'll build friendships, and when you'll pray. As you go through the week, encourage your Jigsaw to check off the days.

Superballs

Checklist? Who needs a stinkin' checklist? Your Superball will be delighted to discover that the four habits that help us grow in our friendship with Jesus work while on the move, too.

Ask your Superball to stay strong this week by sharing his or her faith story with a new friend, or praying while riding a bike or shooting hoops or playing sports, then report back to you how it went.

Teddy Bears

Your Teddy Bear will appreciate the habits, but it's likely that your child will appreciate time with you even more.

Don't rush through your daily time together. Come in rested, and be patient and attentive. Ask your Teddy Bear to help identify the appropriate fellowship-building activity, and to suggest a Bible story or passage to read. Keep in mind that as you disciple your Teddy Bear you're not only drawing your child closer to Jesus...you and your child are growing closer, too.

Your Teddy Bear will love that.

habits...how positive you are about diving into God's Word...those speak volumes to your child.

What priority do you place on growing as a disciple, on staying strong? How can you help your child make it a priority, too?

Where does your child need help standing strong?

Pray:

Dear God, we parents have a weak spot—our kids. I want what's best for my child and I know that's you. I want my child to care about a relationship with you. Please teach me to find strength, not fear, in allowing that relationship to form as you lead it. And Lord, please use me to teach my child that you're what matters most. Amen.

"IN THE CONFRONTATION BETWEEN THE STREAM AND THE ROCK, THE STREAM ALWAYS WINS – NOT THROUGH STRENGTH, BUT BY PERSEVERANCE."

—Anonymous

SESSION 9

Living the Adventure

Following Jesus is a huge adventure that lasts forever! You and your child will look ahead at what's next as Jesus' disciples.

A note from Grant

Adventure: an unusual, exciting experience. The sort of high-energy life portrayed in action movies and on television.

But our lives—waking up, going to work, spending time at church, eating pizza—is that a life of adventure?

It most certainly is.

We disciples live a life packed with excitement and adventure because we never know what God has in store for us. The Bible says that Jesus came to give us a rich, abundant life, and he definitely delivers. There are abundant questions, and a life following Jesus is full of wonder, surprises, and joy. We never know when he'll send us on a mission across the street or around the world.

In short, it's a life of adventure.

Children are far more open to adventure than most adults. "Childlike"-ness goes a long way toward finding adventure in daily life.

Not everything needs to be a thrill ride, but consider: if you aren't finding some adventure in your life, are you following Jesus closely? His goal is to lead his disciples not necessarily where we feel comfortable, but where he wants to go. If there's nothing unexpected in life any longer, perhaps we've quit following.

Embrace discipleship. Embrace adventure.

The Point:

Disciples have exciting lives as they follow Jesus.

What you'll need:

A clean cloth blindfold
A map of your country
Pencils
Your Prayer Notebooks
Piece of your child's favorite candy

Discipler Tip

Look for teachable moments. If a light bulb pops on over your child's head because he or she grasps a new idea, stop and talk about it. The lessons learned during your discipling time need to stay with your child forever (literally!), so don't rush. If a session takes an extra 30 minutes, it's time well spent.

Dive In

Listen Up (20 minutes)

Before beginning this activity, hide a piece of your child's favorite candy where it's not visible—but your child will be able to reach it. Don't give your child any clues where the candy might be lurking!

Say: **I hid a piece of candy I know you like. If you can find it, it's yours. I won't tell you where it is, but I'll lead you to it.**

The trick to this is that you won't be able to see where you're going.

Help your child secure the blindfold in place.

Say: **Can you see me? No? Great—you shouldn't be able to see anything. But if you listen to my voice and do what I say, the candy will be yours in no time.**

Lead your child to the candy, describing any obstacles in the way. Explain how to avoid the obstacles and, when you reach the candy, tell your child how to retrieve it from the hiding place.

Take a roundabout path to the candy; you'll later ask your child about how it felt to rely on your instructions.

Once the candy is retrieved, ask your child to take off the blindfold and talk with you as he or she enjoys the candy.

Ask:

- **What made it difficult to find the candy? Easy?**
- **When did you most feel like taking off your blindfold?**
- **What would have changed had I steered you into a wall?**
- **What about this experience made it an adventure?**

Say: **Notice this: you were in your own home. You were being directed by someone who loves you and who you could trust. You knew at the end of the experience you'd get your favorite candy.**

What made this an adventure was that you ran into some unexpected things along the way. You took some turns you may not have expected.

Being a disciple is a lot like that experience.

- **How do you think it might be the same? different?**

Say: **As disciples, we know where we're going: Heaven. We know whose voice to follow: Jesus' voice. We know pretty much what he wants us to do.**

What makes life an adventure is that he often asks us to do something unexpected. To talk with someone we don't know, or go somewhere new, or give something away that we value. Or to be blessed in ways we never expected.

Do you want to have a boring life? Me either! I'd rather have as much adventure as I can with God guiding me through and keeping me safe.

Ask your child to read 1 Corinthians 10:13 aloud.

Say: **God promises he'll never hit us with something we can't handle with his help.**

He also promised to give us an abundant life. An abundant life is a life full of love and joy, experiences and unknowns. Disciples get a life of adventure, not some boring life that just anyone could have!

Read Psalm 119:105 aloud. If your child is able, ask your child to read the passage.

With your child, discuss:

- **God's Word lights the path for our feet, but it only lights up the pathway a little ahead of where we are. We can't see everything that's coming. How do you feel about that?**

Say: **It takes trust to follow Jesus when we're only shown a step at a time. It takes practice to hear his direction.**

But disciples get steadily better at both seeing and hearing the direction Jesus sends us! Practice helps us enjoy the adventure more!

Dig In

Planes, Trains, and Automobiles

Place a map of your country on the table in front of you and your child. Find your current location on the map. Circle it.

Say: **Here we are. What point on this map looks farthest away to you?**

Circle the point your child chooses as furthest away.

Say: **Let's pretend to travel there. You're in charge of your trip and I'm in charge of mine. We can each pick the way we want to travel, and the route there, so pick the one that's the most fun. Or the most direct. It's up to you.**

You could ride on a train. You could drive yourself. You could take a bus to New York, hop a boat to England, fly a plane to China, then swim until you hit land and pogo stick the rest of the way. It's your call.

Jot your ideas in the back of your Prayer Notebook as you think about it. You'll have three minutes to decide your route and methods of transportation.

I'll work on my notes at the same time.

Take care to come up with an unpredictable route and odd methods of transportation (riding a kangaroo? a llama?) so you and your child have wildly differing solutions to reaching your destination.

Compare plans when three minutes have passed.

Say: **Looks like we're both going to end up the same place—but we're taking way different routes to get there!**

Being a disciple of Jesus is the same way. Those who love and follow Jesus end up in Heaven, but God gives us different adventures on the way there.

Some disciples live here in our town. Others are sent overseas to be missionaries. Some get to Heaven quickly. Others serve on earth for eighty years or more.

Still, we're all going to the same place. The adventure is in the journey.

Read Matthew 4:18-20 aloud. If your child is able, have your child read the passage.

Say: **Peter was a fisherman. He grew up knowing he'd be a fisherman his whole life, doing what his father did for a living.**

Then something changed.

Jesus came along. And instead of being a fisherman, Peter became a fisher of men. An entirely new direction—but one that let him follow Jesus.

Peter's story is like the story of the other disciples in the Bible. When Jesus said, "Here's what I want you do," all of them said, "Okay."

Discuss the following with your child:

- **If you were in Peter's sandals, would you say "okay" to Jesus—even though you didn't know what he had planned for you?**
- **Are you someone who likes surprises—or do you like everything to go according to plan?**

Say: **As disciples, we're on an adventure as we love, follow, and serve Jesus. We're his to direct, his to use. What a great thing!**

Make It Mine

Nothing Ad-ventured, Nothing Gained

Say: **Keep an eye out for signs of adventure this week. If a new person introduces himself, ask yourself how God can use that encounter. If you catch a movie, think about what God might want you to learn from it. Look for God's creative hand in everyone and everything. When something unexpected happens, look for the way that God is moving in your life through it.**

> "Life is either a daring adventure or nothing. Security does not exist in nature, nor do the children of men as a whole experience it. Avoiding danger is no safer in the long run than exposure."
>
> —Helen Keller

Discuss with your child:

• Sometimes life seems pretty routine and dull. Go to school, clean your room, eat dinner, clean your room, go to bed, clean your room. But unexpected things can happen—and when they do, we often feel more alive, more interested in what's happening around us.

• What's something unexpected that happened to you recently? Maybe it's a little thing—but you didn't see it coming.

• What might you learn from that experience?

This week look for unexpected lessons in your own life, and share them with your child. Seeing parents take seriously the challenge of shifting perspective will make doing the same a priority for your child.

Blessed to be a Blessing

Following Jesus is a huge adventure.

At least, it should be.

Consider: when you're taking your family on a trip—across town or across the country—it's usually a goal to plan well. To know where you'll go, how you'll get there, and what you can expect along the way. Nailing down the details is the best way to save time, save money, and avoid surprises.

> "In his heart a man plans his course, but the LORD determines his steps."
>
> —Proverbs 16:9

But God has all the time in the world—and beyond. And money's no problem; he ultimately owns it all. And he's not much concerned about surprising us—he's calling the shots.

Like it or not, you're just along for the ride. When we're following Jesus, there are regularly times we need to be flexible and take a sudden left turn. Our lives are truly not our own.

What God is looking to instill in your child—and you—is a burning, passionate relationship with him. A desire to love and obey him.

And a high tolerance for left turns.

Look for opportunities to do some things out of the ordinary this week. There's a good chance God put them there.

Pray:

Dear God, sometimes unexpected things happen and I feel too tired to appreciate them, or the only unexpected things I notice look a lot like the wheels falling off my life. Please help me change my perspective and clearly see your hand at work. Help me to view my life as you see it, and give me desire to walk through this adventure. To live this abundant life. And I pray for the same view to be part of my child's life, God. Amen.

Think Ahead

If you're attending a Closing Celebration next week, be sure to take your baton with you.

Shifting Perspective

Objective: This week you'll practice seeing your daily lives from God's perspective: as days you're "on call" and at God's disposal at all times. Part of that process is for you and your child to stretch beyond your daily habits.

Jigsaw Puzzles

Jigsaws tend to value routine, so even minor changes can be disruptive. Set the bar low; ask your child to go to school or a friend's house a different way. Ask your child, while on the new route, to pray for people she passes. These are people she'd have never seen had she not stepped outside her routine.

Superballs

No problem asking for Superballs to change things up; they live for adventure! Give your Superball this assignment: to meet 10 new people this week. Point out that meeting new people won't happen if your Superball does the same things he usually does, goes the same place he usually goes, sits with the same friends he always shares lunch with at school.

Ask him to pray for opportunities to engage with new faces, and after meeting and speaking with each new person to silently pray, "God, how would you like me to serve this person?"

Teddy Bears

Some children find diving into new relationships daunting. If your child is one of them, walk through the process with your child. Spend a morning or afternoon together visiting places where people tend to relax and chat with people nearby: a coffee shop, a swimming pool, a community gathering. Even breaking out of the mold and sitting in a different part of the church sanctuary on Sunday morning!

Ask your Teddy Bear to silently pray for each new person he or she meets, asking God, "How can I serve this person? Why have you brought this specific person into my life?"

SESSION 10

Making a Memory

Deciding to become a committed disciple is a huge moment in your child's life. You and your child will make that decision one to remember!

A note from Grant

Think back to your growing-up years at home. If you're like me, most days made very little lasting impression. You and your parent or parents got up, did what you did all day, went to bed. The days blend together.

But that daddy-daughter dance your father took you to? The special camping trip? That time just you and your mom went out shopping for school clothes and you laughed uncontrollably when you tried on matching outfits? Those days stand out as special memory-makers—and you'll treasure them forever.

This week, create one of those memories with your child, honoring him or her for seeing the discipling program through. For making a serious commitment to Jesus, choosing to be a disciple, and then doing something about it.

Have a great time together doing something your child enjoys. Something your child will talk about forever.

When I wanted to give my daughter Megan a special memory, I loaded her and four friends into a rented stretch limo. We first visited a local Emergency Room where a friend of mine met them to serve them before-dinner drinks: Mello-Yello™ in specimen cups. Then the limo whisked us off to a McDonald's where several co-conspirators—wearing tuxes—greeted the ladies and took their orders. Then it was a game of miniature golf.

Several friends joined my daughter Emily for a dinner out and a carriage ride in a picture-perfect town nearby.

And my son, Matthew? Somehow I was able to score a skybox to watch Michael Jordan play one of his last games for the Chicago Bulls. I took Matthew and one of his friends—they're still talking about it.

What would make an incredible memory for your child? Would your child enjoy it most just with you, or would inviting a friend along make it even more special? Is the anticipation something your child

The Point:

Deciding to follow Jesus is a Very Big Deal—and a decision to celebrate!

enjoys, or should you make it a surprise?

Whatever you do—and to be special it doesn't have to be expensive, by the way—consider how much fun you've had just spending time with your child through this discipling program.

Don't let that intimacy you're feeling slip away. Plug a regular time to be together into both your schedules.

And a word to the wise: bring tissues even if you're planning to have a blast at this party. If you're like me, you'll be moved to tears as you consider what God has done in the life of your child.

If you won't attend a Closing Celebration as part of a group, this is your last discipling meeting—and a great time to do some review, to pray for and bless your child, and to pass along your baton.

Dive In

Par-tay!

The goal this week isn't to spend lots of money, but "having fun with child = spending money" is a common equation. That's why we cautioned you early on to set aside money for this outing.

Special outings are often special because you can't afford to do them often. "Let's go catch a ball game" sounds great until you start adding up tickets, parking, snacks, and toss in a souvenir program.

So hopefully by now you have a budget. And you know what you want to do with your child. You've purchased any tickets you need, made whatever reservations you require, cleared the calendar so you and your child are both available.

Or...not.

Maybe you're *still* not sure yet what to do to create a positive memory-maker, a "boy, I remember when..." moment.

If you're still scrambling, relax: there are plenty of options. And it doesn't necessarily have to cost a fortune. Remember: what makes it truly fun is that you're doing it *together*. And that at some point you make eye contact, tell your child how proud you are of him or her, and you then talk about how the past few weeks have changed you both.

A quick list of inexpensive suggestions ends this chapter. Review them if you're still unsure what might make a memorable time together, and you need a spark to ignite your own ideas.

If you won't attend a Closing Celebration as part of a group, this is your last discipling meeting—and a great time to do some review, to pray for and bless your child, and to pass along your baton.

Another special part of your time together this week is praying a blessing over your child. The practice was commonplace in Bible times, and it's just as powerful today.

Review

Before you pick up your child's friends to join in your adventure together, while you and your child are alone, discuss the following:

- **What will you remember from this discipling experience ten years from now?**
- **If you could spend more time on any part of this discipling process, what would it be? What would you want to do?**
- **What part of the past few months felt challenging to you? Why?**
- **What directions do you think Jesus is taking you as you follow him?**

Pray a blessing over your child

Another special part of your time together this week is praying a blessing over your child. The practice was commonplace in Bible times, and it's just as powerful today.

This discipling process has helped you see your child in a new light. Perhaps you've marveled at how your child is growing. You've caught glimpses of how God can use your child to honor himself, and to touch the world.

Blessing your child is simply letting your child hear what you've discovered—and feel the deep joy of hearing how he's valued by God, and by you.

Your child will feel loved, cherished, and precious. And you'll feel the love of God flow through you into the life of your child.

It's probably a good idea to pray the blessing for your child when his or her friends aren't around. Make this an intimate, connected moment by facing your child, making eye contact, and telling your child how proud of him or her you are. And don't let your words be forgotten; write down the blessing you share and tuck it into your baton.

Lay a hand on your child's head. If God has given you any insight into your child's unique abilities and character this past few months, thank God for those gifts. Name them, and ask God to use them now and in the future.

Share the prayer requests you've written during the past few months with your child. For my daughter Megan, I prayed that she grow in her faith and be a faithful follower of Jesus as an adult, that she marry a Christian, and that she serve the Lord full-time.

All prayers that were answered in the affirmative!

Pass the baton

In the baton, place a copy of the Covenant you downloaded (if you're going to a Closing Celebration, a copy will be provided for you). Include the prayer requests you've written, and a copy of the blessing you shared.

Say: **I want you to have this symbol of our discipling time together. It's my prayer that you'll continue to grow in your relationship with Jesus, and that you'll disciple other people. The covenant we signed doesn't have an ending date—we're disciples of Jesus forever.**

I'm proud of you for the commitment you've put into this past few months. Let's continue to pray specifically, to be in fellowship, to read and live out God's Word, and to share our faith stories. Those are habits we can enjoy our entire lives.

Pray together

Together, thank Jesus for his powerful example, for his love, for calling you to be his followers. Pledge to him your hearts now and forever.

Ideas for your night out!

- **Take a nature walk** at the local park or beach. Bring along bread to feed whatever birds decide you owe it to them.
- **Visit a Bonsai specialty store** and learn how to trim a Bonsai. Buy a plant and with it as your centerpiece at a restaurant, talk about how God is shaping and trimming you, too.
- **Bowling**—but make it special by using only your less dominant hand. Righties bowl leftie, lefties bowl rightie. See if you can break 25.
- **Spend the evening at an amusement park.** Go on whatever rides your child chooses.
- **Take a few laps at a go-cart track.** Look ahead to your child's driving years with trepidation.
- **Window shop in an exclusive shopping area.** Try things on. Decide how you'd accessorize if budget were no problem—and then let your child pick out something special (up to your pre-set amount!).
- **Visit the zoo.** See if there's an event at the zoo, like an art show or musical performance. Don't feed the animals. Do feed your child.
- **Go to a local festival or specialty show.** Monster truck rally, anyone?
- **A movie,** but not just any movie. Go to an Imax!
- **Arrange for a hot air balloon ride.** You won't know exactly where you'll land, but you'll have a great time getting there!
- **Line up a quick trip in a private plane** so you can see where you live from the sky.
- **Attend a concert.** Hopefully something you both enjoy—it won't be any fun for your child if you sit through the entire show with your hands over your ears screaming, "turn it down!"
- **Kick back at a rodeo.**
- **Play a round of miniature golf**...with the putters upside down.

SESSION 11

Optional Launch Party

If a group of you are doing this program together, start out with a fun event that sets the vision and builds support. Here's how to do it!

A note from Grant

If you're like me, you're great on seeing the value of a new program or project. It's *completing* things that gets in my way. I can always think of one more thing to do...but they don't all get finished.

You might be concerned that you'll jump into this discipling program and then, about week three, just let it slide. Either you or your child will lose enthusiasm and it'll fizzle away to nothing.

I can guarantee that once you start a discipling relationship you'll hit some snags. That's because what you're doing is so important that the enemy will try to stop you. You'll run into scheduling snafus. Get called out of town on business. Something will come up—and that's just an indication of how important this program really is in the life of your child.

So do this: stack the deck in your favor.

Get others involved. Ask your Children's Ministry Director or Pastor to help you find other parents who want to have a similar experience with their children and tackle the discipling program as a group.

Consider how many times you or parents you know have launched into a program with a child, only to have it fizzle. A Cub Scout who never makes it past Webelos. A Brownie Scout who doesn't last past the first cookie drive. A camper who wears out long before his or her sleeping bag.

You need the support and accountability that comes with having a group if there's any way your church (or you personally) can pull one together.

What You'll Need:

Chairs

A way to play music—CD player, sound system, etc.

Nametags

Batons—one per adult

1 Bible

1 copy of the Covenant for each guest, plus an extra copy

1 copy of First Steps for each adult guest

Red inkpad

Black or blue pens

Party food—cupcakes, punch, cake, ice cream and toppings, etc.

Here's how it works

After advertising the program, your church will host a Launch Party for parents and children who want to do this program. It doesn't matter if there are two sets of parents and kids or twenty—the support is worth the effort of launching this party.

Then, as you disciple your child, tap into the network of other parents for support and accountability. Pray for each other.

On week 12, get back together for a wrap-up celebration.

It's that easy.

If you're a church leader, I encourage you to call parents every few weeks to see how the discipling is going. There's great power in accountability, and in the ceremonies used in this launch party and the closing celebration.

Besides, it's more fun when you're on a team!

Get ready...Get set...

What fun is a party with no guests?

Long before your launch party, advertise the discipling program so parents of other children know it's available. Describe the program through your church communications. Spread the word personally.

We're assuming that if you're doing a launch party that this discipling program is part of your church's children or family ministry. With that in mind, the following instructions are intended for whoever is hosting the party.

And go!

Select a room for your meeting that's about full when the expected number of people are in it. It's discouraging to have a small circle of chairs in the corner of a gymnasium; it appears that nobody came!

Place chairs in a circle—just the number you think you need. Have extras handy; if more people come you can always quickly enlarge the circle.

Play some upbeat instrumental music as guests arrive. This is a party, after all! Just make sure that the music doesn't overpower the possibility of discussion, and that your musical choice is something most people enjoy.

As guests arrive, ask everyone to fill out a name tag.

On the tag ask each guest to write his or her first and last name, and—in the upper left-hand corner—to write one place in life the guest got lost. It may have been on a trip, or while finding a classroom in a new school; anywhere it happened is fine.

When it's time to begin, slowly turn down the music and ask guests to make note of the person who's directly across the circle. That person will be a partner for the next exercise. If there's an odd number of people, jump in to be a partner.

Story Time! (15 minutes)

Ask guests to briefly share the "lost" stories hinted at on their name tags with their partners. Each partner should talk for up to 60 seconds.

And it's important that partners listen carefully—guests will tell their partner's story to a larger group!

If you have more than eight people at your launch party, have pairs join up with other pairs to form foursomes and tell their partners' stories there. That way everyone can talk, and it won't take a half-hour to get through the stories.

If you have eight or fewer guests, give each guest 45 seconds to tell his or her partner's story of woe about being lost. What happened? How did it end? Is the partner still lost somewhere on the highway or in the wilderness?

Voiceprint (up to 25 minutes)

Ask children to stand in the circle.

Say: **I'd like each parent to stand behind his or her child. Children, please close your eyes—and keep them closed. Parents, in a moment I'll ask you to take hold of your child's shoulders and spin your child in a circle several times. Your child should feel a bit dizzy and disoriented about which way he or she is facing, but don't let anyone take a nosedive to the floor. Ready? Go.**

While parents are spinning their children, remove a chair from the circle and stand away from the "hole" in your circle of chairs.

Say: **Parents, once you're certain your child is steady, step away from your child and join me outside the circle. Kids, keep your eyes closed.**

After parents exit, have them wait silently with you.

Say: **Kids, keep your eyes closed. In a moment I'm going to ask one of the parents to ask you to come toward his or her voice. Only come if you know it's your parent. Everyone else will stay still.**

Parents, when you call your children, don't use your kids' names. Just keep talking so your child knows where you are and can move toward you.

Kids, you may bump and thump against someone else while you're coming, so walk slowly with your arms out in front of you. When you reach your parent, you'll be greeted with a hug.

Here's the first parent.

Signal for a parent to stand in the "hole" and begin speaking.

After each parent has had a turn, and collected his or her child, have guests silently return to the circle and move their chairs so parents are facing their own children.

Ask your teams of parents and kids to discuss:

- **Children, how did it feel to make your way to your parents?**
- **Parents, how did it feel to be guiding your children? To see that your children were blindly moving where they could trip and fall?**
- **What made it difficult or easy to recognize the voice of a parent?**

Read aloud John 10:1-5; 11-15. The New Living Translation version is printed below for your convenience.

"I tell you the truth, anyone who sneaks over the wall of a sheepfold, rather than going through the gate, must surely be a thief and a robber! But the one who enters through the gate is the shepherd of the sheep.

"The gatekeeper opens the gate for him, and the sheep recognize his voice and come to him. He calls his own sheep by name and leads them out. After he has gathered his own flock, he walks ahead of them, and they follow him because they know his voice. They won't follow a stranger; they will run from him because they don't know his voice.

"I am the good shepherd. The good shepherd sacrifices his life for the sheep.

"A hired hand will run when he sees a wolf coming. He will abandon the sheep because they don't belong to him and he isn't their shepherd. And so the wolf attacks them and scatters the flock. The hired hand runs away because he's working only for the money and doesn't really care about the sheep.

"I am the good shepherd; I know my own sheep, and they know me, just as my Father knows me and I know the Father. So I sacrifice my life for the sheep."

Say: **What Jesus described is like what just happened with us.**

You kids were in a "sheepfold," an enclosure with just one opening. And you only came out when you heard a familiar voice, the voice of someone who loves you.

Nobody had to tell you whose voice to follow. You knew the voice of your parent.

During the next few months we'll learn to recognize Jesus' voice, too. To know how to follow him closely. That's what disciples do: they follow Jesus and let him slowly and thoroughly change how they think, feel, and act.

Parents, as you lead weekly sessions you'll become better disciples along with your children. All of us can grow in following Jesus. None of us is perfect.

This will be an adventure for everyone!

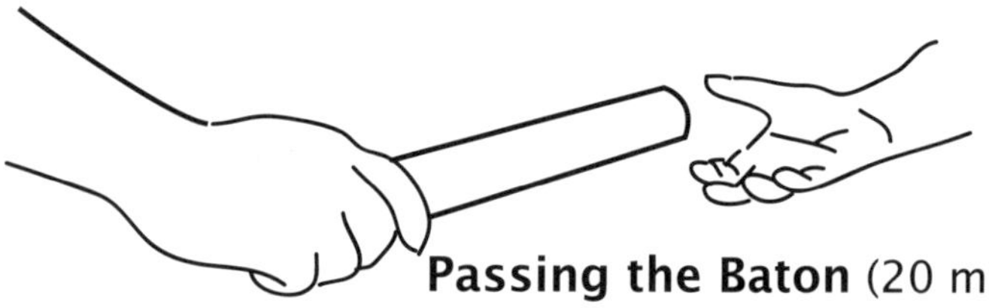

Passing the Baton (20 minutes)

Say: **You'll launch your first session this coming week. You parents are responsible for picking a time where you and your child have 45 minutes of focused, relaxed time together. It may be hard to find—but it's important!**

There will be some work to do together. Activities to do, discussions to have, some verses to learn. All of it is important—please don't skip anything.

In fact, if you'd like more opportunity to dig into what you're learning, visit the Discipling Another to Love Jesus website at www.disciplinganother.com and download art starts, movie connects, and games.

No information is collected at the site, so it's safe for kids to visit. And all the downloads are free.

Your next step is to decide if this is what you really want to do. If you're serious about becoming a more faithful follower of Jesus. It's a big decision.

I hope you've talked about it before this meeting, but if not—now is your chance.

I'm going to ask you all to sign a Covenant of Discipleship.

Pass out text copies to each person. Keep the more formal copy next to you, lying across an open Bible.

Say: **This Covenant outlines what you'll do in the coming weeks. Listen carefully and follow along as I read the Covenant to you.**

Read aloud the Covenant. Don't read the verses in parentheses.

When you've finished, ask parents and children to again sit facing each other. Give them several minutes to discuss:

- **How will going through this experience together be a good thing in our lives?**

• **What might get in the way of our doing this? How can we overcome those obstacles?**

Say: **If you'd like to launch into this discipleship adventure together, please come up and sign your names on this Covenant. And when you've finished signing, place your thumb on the red inkpad and put your fingerprint over your name.**

If you've decided to not do this discipleship adventure at this time, please stay seated.

After everyone who wants to covenant together has done so, hold up a *First Steps: Discipling Your Child* book and a silver baton.

Say: **This book is for each adult. It outlines the sessions you'll lead in the coming weeks. And you'll also get one of these: a baton. Please keep your baton someplace your family will see it often—on the kitchen table, on the television set, by the computer.**

At track events there's often a relay race that uses a baton. One runner dashes around the track and then hands the baton to the next runner, who also does a lap. Each time the baton is passed along it's up to that new runner to carry it.

We've all received a baton. Jesus sent his disciples out into the world to share the good news of his life, death, and resurrection. That good news was passed from one person to another, to another, to another...and now here we are. We've also received it.

Each of you adults will now receive a book and a baton. Your job, over the next few months, is to intentionally share what you've learned about being a disciple with your child. You'll pass the baton.

Along the way you'll learn things, too, because you're still growing as a disciple. We're all in the race—and we've all got things to learn.

Pass a book and baton to each adult.

Say: **Remember: keep this baton where you'll see it daily. Let it be a reminder of the important work you're doing as you disciple your child.**

For your convenience, a copy of the downloadable Covenant is printed on page 97. Feel free to make copies for your local church use.

Closing Prayer (2 minutes)

Make this a prayer of dedication—asking God to bless each discipling relationship as it unfolds.

Party Snacks!

It ain't a party until the cookies, cake, or ice cream hit the table. Bring out munchies and party foods and encourage guests to chat and celebrate what God will be doing in and through them.

Verses:

Developing obedience

Mark 12:28–31, Deuteronomy 30:19–20, Romans 12:1

Invite other believers into friendships

Proverbs 17:17, Hebrews 10:24–25, 1 John 3:11

Study the Bible

Joshua 1:8, 2 Timothy 3:16–17, James 1:21, James 1:25

Consistently make good choices

Proverbs 1:7, James 1:5, Ephesians 4:1, Colossians 3:1

Impact others with my faith story

Philemon 6 (NIV), Matthew 28:19–20, Colossians 4:5–6

Pray regularly

Matthew 7:7, 1 Thessalonians 5:17, James 5:17

Learn to stay strong

Nehemiah 8:10, Ephesians 6:10, James 4:7

Experience the adventure of following Jesus...forever

John 15:15, Romans 8:14, Galatians 5:25

Covenant

I want to grow as a disciple, so to the best of my ability I will...

Develop loving obedience (Matthew 28:19–20)
Invite other believers into friendships (Hebrews 10:24–25)
Study the Bible (2 Timothy 3:16–17)
Consistently make good choices (Ephesians 4:1)
Impact others with my faith story (Colossians 4:5–6)
Pray regularly—and specifically (Matthew 7:7)
Learn to stay strong (Ephesians 6:10)
Experience the adventure of following Jesus—forever! (Galatians 5:25)

Permission to copy granted for local church use. © Discipling Another to Love Jesus

SESSION 12

Optional Celebration Party

You made it! This closing celebration party is a wrap-up for your group's discipling adventure. It's icing on the cake—and that sounds like a party to us!

A note from Grant

Many years ago, I worked as a lifeguard.

When I first started, I figured my job was to sit on a little tower looking bronzed and authoritative, scanning the water for drowning people. When I saw someone splashing around in a panic I'd then leap into action, paddling on out to perform a heroic rescue.

It didn't take long for more experienced lifeguards to set me straight.

A good lifeguard doesn't wait for trouble before acting. He prevents trouble by being proactive, by looking for who's heading into unsafe water and intervening early.

Discipling young believers is a lot like that.

You've just proactively helped one young believer—your child—by helping your child grow closer to Jesus. By helping your child become a more intentional disciple.

But there are other kids out there heading toward unsafe water, too. Kids who are facing life without a deeply rooted relationship with Jesus. Maybe those children live in your home; maybe they're children in your church. Maybe they're in the homes of your friends.

You're now a trained lifeguard. Would you consider discipling another child? There's a need—and you've got experience. Talk with the Christian Education Director at your church about how you might safely connect with other children.

Even better—talk with Christian parents whose children haven't yet been discipled. Share your experiences. Reassure parents that they can have a powerful experience with their kids, the same way you've enjoyed one with yours.

Good disciplers are like good lifeguards: they act before people get in serious trouble.

Don't wait until kids are struggling. Act now.

What You'll Need:

Chairs

A way to play music—CD player, sound system, etc.

Name tags

Batons—one per adult

1 color copy of the signed Covenant for each guest

Ice cream sundae supplies: several flavors of ice cream, whipped cream, bananas, toppings such as coconut, nuts, chocolate sauce, caramel sauce, etc.

Get ready...Get set...

Long before this Celebration Party, remind your discipling parent/child pairs that it's coming. That there will be some special moments in the party they won't want to miss.

And do this: if you're a church leader who will use this program again, invite parents who are considering going through this experience with their children. Let them see what the impact has been, hear stories from the people who've just completed the program.

The following instructions assume you're hosting the party.

And go!

Like your Launch Party, select a room for your meeting that's about full when the expected number of people are in it.

Place chairs in a circle—just the number you think you need. Have extras handy; if more people come you can always quickly enlarge the circle.

Play some upbeat instrumental music as guests arrive. Select music that most people enjoy. No polka just because you're a fan!

As guests arrive, ask everyone to fill out a name tag.

On the tag ask each guest to write his or her first and last name, and—in the upper left-hand corner—to write his or her favorite ice cream flavor...the more specific, the better. For example, Rocky Road, chocolate with almonds, vanilla bean, etc.

Encourage parents and kids to share stories about their Week 10 evenings. Both adults and kids will enjoy telling about the fun they had!

Ice Cream Convincing (15 minutes)

When it's time to begin, slowly turn down the music and ask guests to stand and find someone who shares a taste for a different ice cream flavor. When they've connected, have them pause while you give instructions.

Say: **Take 30 seconds to decide which person in your pair has a birthday closest to the third Sunday in July. That's National Ice Cream Day in America.**

Pause to let pairs figure it out.

Say: **If you had the birthday closest to National Ice Cream Day, you'll now have 60 seconds to convince your partner that your flavor of ice cream is better than the flavor the other person wrote on his or her nametag. Your goal is to win over your partner to your way of thinking.**

Ready to try? Go.

After 60 seconds have partners switch roles and do the activity again.

When the time is up, have guests return to their seats and turn their chairs so they can talk with their discipling partner.

Ask partners to discuss:

- **What strategies did the other person use to try to convince you to change your loyalty to your favorite flavor?**
- **How well did the other person's arguments work?**
- **Did you change your mind? Why or why not?**

Allow time for discussion, then draw attention back to yourself.

Say: **What you just experienced is a lot like what happens in the world regarding our faith. As a disciple of Jesus, you can expect lots of people to try to change your mind. To change your loyalty to Jesus.**

You may be told that believing in Jesus is silly. That it's for babies. That you're not open-minded unless you also try following someone or something other than Jesus.

But here's something that nobody can argue: *your experience.*

If you've learned to hear Jesus' voice and felt his love, nobody can argue that. It's *real.* It's your *experience.* You can stand firm in your loving relationship with Jesus, no matter what.

Your faith story is just that: *your* faith story. You can share it with the confidence that comes from knowing it's true.

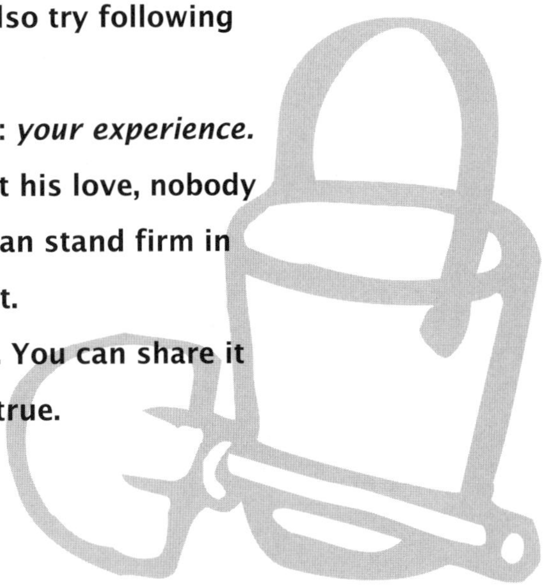

Put the questions on a PowerPoint slide and project it, or make copies of the questions so discipling pairs don't have to write them down.

Talk About It (20 minutes)

Ask parents to hold the batons they brought with them.

Say: **A few months ago you were given your baton as a reminder that, by discipling your child, you're passing along something special to your child. You were helping your child know, love, and follow Jesus. To hear Jesus' voice and obey it.**

Here's what I expect really happened: as you worked through the discipling you both received something.

You both grew in your faith. You both grew in your love for Jesus. You both enjoyed having more time than usual together.

I'd like you two to talk about what happened during this discipling process.

For the next 15 minutes, relax and discuss:

- **What do you think you'll remember from this discipling experience ten years from now?**
- **If you could spend more time on any part of this discipling process, what would it be? What would you want to do?**
- **What part of the past few months felt challenging to you? Why?**
- **What directions do you think Jesus is taking you as you follow him?**

Passing the Baton ... again (15 minutes)

Draw attention to yourself.

Say: **I've made copies of the Covenant we signed when we met the first time. I'd like each discipler to come pick one up and then go back to your seat.**

Distribute the copies, and then—when everyone is seated—ask both disciplers and the children who've been discipled to hold their copy and bow their heads in prayer.

Pray: **Dear God, thank you for the past weeks of discipling. We know we're not done, that following you is a lifelong process. Right here, right now, we commit ourselves to listening for your voice, and going where you lead. To the best of our abilities, we will be your followers all our days. Amen.**

Ask adults to roll up their Covenant and place it in the baton.

Then ask each child and adult to take an end of the adult's baton and not let it go until you tell them to do so.

Say: **Now, disciplers, please pray for the child you discipled. Pray specifically, asking God for what you believe your child will need in order to be a faithful follower of Jesus.**

I'll close for us.

When most adults have finished praying, pray:

Dear God, you alone know the future. You know what the children here need to become ever stronger followers of your Son, Jesus. You are good, God, and we know you love these children even more than we do. Make them yours forever, God. Give them the challenges that will shape them and bring compassion into their lives. Give them the direction that will keep them ever following your Son. These disciples are yours, God. Amen.

Adults, please release your end of the baton.

That baton now belongs to you, kids. It has been passed to you, and is yours to keep all your life as a reminder that you are a follower of Jesus. That you are a disciple. And that you, too, can disciple another person to love Jesus.

Kids, please come up now and get another baton. Take it with you back to your seat.

Give each child a new baton. Once children are seated, ask each child and adult to take an end of the new baton and not let it go until you tell them to do so. Then ask that children and adults bow their heads.

Say: **Those of you who were discipled, please pray for the person who discipled you. Pray for that person specifically. Thank God for that person pouring his or her life into yours. For being willing to be an example of a person who tries to hear Jesus and follow Jesus. I'll close for us.**

When most children have finished praying, pray:

Dear God, you show us your love in so many ways. But the way that touches us most deeply is through the love of someone who is willing to share his or her life with us.

Thank you for the parents who have discipled their children. Thank you that you have worked in and through them. Thank you that you will continue to work in and through them as they grow in faithfully following you. Amen.

Children, please release your end of the baton.

That baton now belongs to you, adults. It's yours as a reminder that you have something to share with new believers. That God has used you and will use you again if you're willing to be used. That you're a disciple—and that you can disciple others to love Jesus.

Please join me in prayer.

Pray: **Dear God, we thank you for this discipling we've experienced. We love you and want to follow you. Thank you for your love, and that you've called us to be more than a fan club or a group of admirers. You've called us to be followers of Jesus. What an honor, God. What a wonderful calling. Bless us as we seek to be ever more faithful. Amen.**

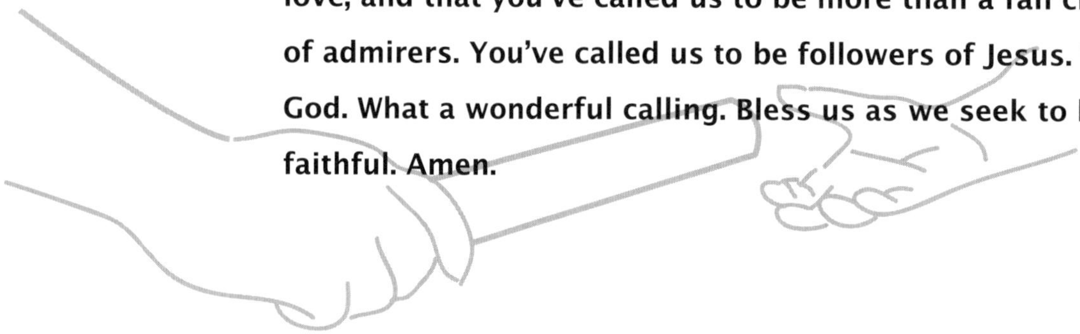

Ice Cream Sundaes (until kids are ready to leave!)

Say: **We don't have every one of your favorite ice creams, but hopefully what we have will be okay.**

I'll bring out the ice cream and toppings. Everyone, please hang out awhile and enjoy talking with each other—and building your favorite ice cream sundae!

Life Issue Verses

1 John 2:16 identifies three major life issues that lead us into sin:

- wanting to please ourselves
- wanting the sinful things we see
- being too proud of what we have (and who we are)

It's likely that one of these three life issues is a common stumbling block for your child. It's not the *only* place your child may trip, but it's where your child stumbles most easily.

Following is a list of common sins that fall in each life issue. Some sins are adult-oriented; we've added them to the list to help you determine which is *your* life issue, too.

Wanting to please ourselves

Lustful thoughts, adultery, overeating, laziness, pornography, sexual addiction and other addictions, willful disobedience.

Wanting the sinful things we see

Materialism, anxiety, depression, financial problems, overspending, selfishness, greed, and failure to keep commitments.

Being too proud of what we have (and who we are)

An unhealthy desire for fame, anger, abuse, control,

"THESE ARE THE WAYS OF THE WORLD: WANTING TO PLEASE OUR SINFUL SELVES, WANTING THE SINFUL THINGS WE SEE, AND BEING TOO PROUD OF WHAT WE HAVE. NONE OF THESE COME FROM THE FATHER, BUT ALL OF THEM COME FROM THE WORLD."

—I John 2:16 (NCV)

This Life Verse activity is designed to give your child tools to address an area of weakness. Providing that training now—while your child is young—is a huge advantage for your child.

gossip, bitterness, selfish ambition, road rage, racism, unbelief, spiritual blindness, skepticism, and seeking the approval of others in unhealthy ways.

Two dangers when looking at the above list with your child in mind:

First, you might think your child can't possibly already have a life issue yet. After all, your child is so young. How can there possibly be something so sinister at work in your child's life?

And second, you might look at the list and feel your stomach sink. You recognize your child in one or more areas; you wonder if somehow it's already too late, if your child is already cemented into a life of ongoing sin.

Relax.

Spiritual growth, like physical growth, is a *dynamic* process. And dealing with sin isn't something your child has to do alone. Remember: God's power is greater than the power of sin. And when your child does sin, God is faithful to forgive when your child repents.

This Life Verse activity is designed to give your child tools to address an area of weakness. Providing that training now—while your child is young—is a huge advantage for your child.

If you and your child can't decide which life issue is most relevant, do this: have your child learn several verses to address each life issue!

If your child struggles with wanting to please him/herself, here are helpful verses:

I hope my words and thoughts please you. Lord, you are my Rock, the one who saves me. —Psalm 19:14 (NCV)

They are blessed whose thoughts are pure, for they will see God. —Matthew 5:8

So now, those who are in Christ Jesus are not judged guilty. —Romans 8:1

So brothers and sisters, since God has shown us great mercy, I beg you to offer your lives as a living sacrifice to him. Your offering must be only for God and pleasing to him, which is the spiritual way for you to worship. —Romans 12:1

But clothe yourselves with the Lord Jesus Christ and forget about satisfying your sinful self. —Romans 13:14

The only temptation that has come to you is that which everyone has. But you can trust God, who will not permit you to be tempted more than you can stand. But when you are tempted, he will also give you a way to escape so that you will be able to stand it. —1 Corinthians 10:13

We have freedom now, because Christ made us free. So stand strong. Do not change and go back into the slavery of the law. —Galatians 5:1

So put out of your life every evil thing and every kind of wrong. Then in gentleness accept God's teaching that is planted in your hearts, which can save you. —James 1:21

So prepare your minds for service and have self-control. All your hope should be for the gift of grace that will be yours when Jesus Christ is shown to you. Now that you are obedient children of God do not live as you did in the past. You did not understand, so you did the evil things you wanted. But be holy in all you do, just as God, the One who called you, is holy. It is written in the Scriptures: "You must be holy, because I am holy." —1 Peter 1:13-16

But if we confess our sins, he will forgive our sins, because we can trust God to do what is right. He will cleanse us from all the wrongs we have done. —1 John 1:9

If your child struggles with wanting the sinful things he or she sees, here are helpful verses:

If you make a promise to give something to the LORD your God, do not be slow to pay it, because the LORD your God demands it from you. Do not be guilty of sin. —Deuteronomy 23:21

Nehemiah said, "Go and enjoy good food and sweet drinks. Send some to people who have none, because today is a holy day to the Lord. Don't be sad, because the joy of the LORD will make you strong." —Nehemiah 8:10

He has put his angels in charge of you to watch over you wherever you go. —Psalm 91:11

Let the peace that Christ gives control your thinking, because you were all called together in one body to have peace. Always be thankful. —Colossians 3:15

So don't worry about tomorrow, because tomorrow will have its own worries. Each day has enough trouble of its own. —Matthew 6:34

Be humble under God's powerful hand so he will lift you up when the right time comes. Give all your worries to him, because he cares about you. —1 Peter 5:6–7

Do not love the world or the things in the world. If you love the world, the love of the Father is not in you. —1 John 2:15

Serving God does make us very rich, if we are satisfied with what we have. We brought nothing into the world, so we can take nothing out. —1 Timothy 6:6–7

God did not give us a spirit that makes us afraid but a spirit of power and love and self-control. —2 Timothy 1:7

The Good News shows how God makes people right with himself—that it begins and ends with faith. As the Scripture says, "But those who are right with God will live by faith." —Romans 1:17

If your child struggles with being too proud of what he or she has and who he or she is, here are helpful verses:

God, you are my God. I search for you. I thirst for you like someone in a dry, empty land where there is no water. —Psalm 63:1

Watch out for your friends, and don't trust your own relatives, because every relative is a cheater, and every friend tells lies about you. Everyone lies to his friend, and no one speaks the truth. The people of Judah have taught their tongues to lie. They have become tired from sinning. —Jeremiah 9:4–5

Be careful of false prophets. They come to you looking gentle like sheep, but they are really dangerous like wolves. You will know these people by what they do. Grapes don't come from thorn bushes, and figs don't come from thorny weeds. —Matthew 7:15–16

And this hope will never disappoint us, because God has poured out his love to fill our hearts. He gave us his love through the Holy Spirit, whom God has given to us. —Romans 5:5

My friends, do not try to punish others when they wrong you, but wait for God to punish them with his anger. It is written: "I will punish those who do wrong; I will repay them," says the Lord. —Romans 12:19

God has made us what we are. In Christ Jesus, God made us to do good works, which God planned in advance for us to live our lives doing. —Ephesians 2:10

My brothers and sisters, when you have many kinds of troubles, you should be full of joy, because you know that these troubles test your faith, and this will give you patience. —James 1:2–3

But God gives us even more grace, as the Scripture says, "God is against the proud, but he gives grace to the humble." —James 4:6

The time is near when all things will end. So think clearly and control yourselves so you will be able to pray. Most importantly, love each other deeply, because love will cause people to forgive each other for many sins. Open your homes to each other, without complaining. —1 Peter 4:7–9

This is how we know what real love is: Jesus gave his life for us. So we should give our lives for our brothers and sisters. —1 John 3:16

FIRST STEPS

Order a copy of the *First Steps* notebook from disciplinganother.com. This notebook will give you a practical tool for one-on-one discipleship.

SWIMMING LESSONS

Order a copy of *Swimming Lessons* from disciplinganother.com. This book explains the foundational principles of one-on-one discipleship. *Swimming Lessons* is a companion to the *First Steps* notebook giving a more in-depth understanding on why and how to disciple.